The Complete Guide to

Creating and Managing New Projects

for Voluntary Organisations

Alan Lawrie

Third edition

DIRECTORY OF SOCIAL CHANGE

Published by
Directory of Social Change
24 Stephenson Way
London NW1 2DP
Tel. 08450 77 77 07; Fax 020 7391 4804
email publications@dsc.org.uk
www.dsc.org.uk
from whom further copies and a full books catalogue are available.

Directory of Social Change Northern Office
Federation House, Hope Street, Liverpool L1 9BW
Policy & Research 0151 708 0136

Directory of Social Change is a Registered Charity no. 800517

First published 1996
Second edition 2006
Third edition 2010

ISBN 978 1 906294 40 3

British Library Cataloguing in Publication Data
A catalogue record for this book is available from the British Library

Cover design by Kate Bass
Text designed by Stephen Strong
Typeset by Marlinzo Services, Frome
Printed and bound by Page Bros, Norwich

Contents

iii

Acknowledgements

The author would like to thank Brian McCausland and Peter Baker for giving freely of their time in reviewing the draft manuscript. Their suggestions and comments were invaluable.

Introduction

In an average year around 9,000 new charities are registered and 115,000 new commercial companies are formed. Throughout the economy new products and services are being introduced at an increasingly fast pace. Despite uncertainties concerning future funding and future prospects, there is continual interest in creating new organisations and new projects.

This book looks at the key decisions and processes involved in starting up a successful project. It is relevant to two types of new project:

- a project set up as an entirely new and independent organisation with its own legal status
- a project created within an existing organisation – this could be a new service, activity or venture.

What is a project?

Often, the term 'project' is used loosely. There are several definitions of what is (and is not) a project. Here are four of the most important features.

1 A project is unique

There should be an idea behind a project that is new, different and innovative. It is not just a copy of what has happened before.

2 A project is time-limited

Projects usually have a limited life. Often, funding or other constraints limit a project's ability to become a permanent organisation.

3 A project creates changes

Projects should have clear plans of what they want to change. There needs to be a vision behind the project. It should make some measurable difference: the changes should last after the project has gone.

4 A project is goal-orientated

A new project needs to have a realistic and achievable plan and strategy to enable it to use all of its efforts to make maximum impact. The way it is managed and organised needs to be goal-orientated.

Sometimes projects lack these features or they are not developed fully. Often, projects have them at the start but lose them as they become more concerned about internal issues and their long-term survival. Projects can very easily stay past their shelf-life.

Projects can be independent or housed in organisations. Planning and managing them requires a different approach to many of the traditional ways in which we have run our organisations. It also needs a willingness to adapt to new ideas.

Do we not have enough projects already?

In the United Kingdom there is an abundance of charities, housing associations, statutory services, self-help groups, not-for-profit agencies and assorted quangos. In England and Wales there are more than 180,000 organisations registered with the Charity Commission. So why spend time creating more projects?

It can appear to be more effective to do something new, and it seems easier to start something new – either inside or outside of an organisation – than to try to change what an existing organisation is doing. Most of the discussions about managing change are about doing new things. However, often the reality is harder. Organisational changes fail not because people do not want to do something new, but because they refuse to give up the old. Many organisational changes are blocked because it seems impossible to stop doing existing things and break with the past. A new organisation or project does not have the history and traditions which can hold a new idea back.

New projects travel lighter

Managed well, new projects can create a new identity, build relationships, operate flexibly and work faster. In an established organisation it is easy for routines, structures and a sense of 'this is how we do it here' to get in the way. A new project can have a focus and vision that is clear and a sense of direction which can unite and excite people. In an established organisation issues of vision, values and direction can become confused. The long-term survival of the organisation and maintenance of the status quo become more important.

It is easier to sell a new project

For different reasons, people who control resources seem attracted to backing new projects rather than providing long-term support to existing ones. This can create a cynical atmosphere, as applicants play a game with funders: applicants automatically use words such as 'innovative' and 'creative' to repackage existing activities. In addition, very few funders are willing to commit themselves to a long-term investment. The National Lottery's distribution boards have funded activities mainly on a project basis.

There is no hard or reliable evidence about the success or failure of new projects in the not-for-profit sector. The evidence from various studies of small businesses suggests that as many as one in five will cease trading within two years of their being established. Market forces can decide their viability easily: if there is no demand for a product the effects will be clearly felt. Feedback from the not-for-profit market, however, is less immediate and not so defined or predictable. Moreover, success is much harder to define. If a charity fails to meet its objectives it is likely that it will struggle to continue, until at some point either it will fade away gradually or become moribund. In the public sector, if a statutory project or programme does not operate as intended, action to remedy it can be late or non-existent, and it is likely that the project will be quietly forgotten. Resources will be taken away from it to be used in another project. Furthermore, a profit test is only appropriate for a commercial company; some not-for-profit projects lack any measurable sense of success or failure.

In researching this book the most useful evidence was anecdotal. I was unable to discover the essential ingredients that would make any new project work. No foolproof recipe on how to start a successful new project is on offer. Often, factors such as chance, serendipity, creative thinking and inspired leadership are crucial to the success of a new project. These factors are frustratingly difficult to package and replicate. However, it is possible to describe the main tasks and processes involved and to suggest techniques and tools which can make the process of starting up an internal and external process easier to manage.

Books that suggest simple formulae to guarantee success are dangerous because many of their case studies are inclined to go through disasters and crises after publication: today's stars often fall. Two things can be learned from this: first, that success is usually only a temporary phenomenon; second, that the critical factors which create success can be lost along the way. However, in the research and discussions for this book, eight features kept cropping up as important issues in creating and managing the successful start-up of a new project.

1 Clarity of purpose

Here, there is a strong sense of vision and values. People involved in the project are focused on making a difference. They have a clear vision of what they want to achieve and the main steps towards it. Vision is the overall sense of what the project aims to do, change and achieve: it is about the difference that the project intends to make. Values are the ethos and principles that underpin the actions taken. Statements of vision and values need to be clear enough to unite people within the project and to explain the project to the outside world.

2 A sense of energy

Activities and work on the project have a feeling of direction and even urgency around them. People want the project to happen and are prepared to run an obstacle course to overcome the barriers and hurdles in their way. The people leading the project need to be able to inspire confidence and communicate the project's vision and values.

3 People think objectively about the project

The people promoting the project regularly stand back and think through their assumptions about the project realistically. They ask, or have to answer, searching and even awkward questions, such as: will it really work? Is it really that new? Will it make a difference? They do not allow their enthusiasm for it to get in the way of dealing with hard issues.

4 It works in an open and participative way

New people are welcome; information is shared. Formal and informal networks of supporters, backers, friends and experts are formed to help the project get off the ground. Many people are encouraged to have a stake in it.

5 A team effort

Often, one or two individuals have a critical role in getting the project up and running, and without them, nothing happens. However, they operate as catalysts by involving and supporting other people. Few individuals have the talents, skills and patience to carry out all of the tasks involved in starting up a new project. The people at the centre of the project seem to operate as leaders and coaches rather than sole performers.

6 A flexible way of working and managing

Decision-making structures, budgets, job descriptions and organisational systems need to be clear, simple and capable of responding quickly to change. A tendency to create bureaucracy and to add structures and overhead costs must be kept in check. New projects need to be able to make decisions quickly, act on them and move resources flexibly. Continuous change and uncertainty is accepted as the norm.

7 A clear identity

A new project needs to have an easily understandable identity and image. What it is for, what it will (or will not) do and what it values need to be presented in such a way that people can understand and pick up the central message quickly. People connected to the project should be able to describe its central ideas in headlines rather than having to write pages.

8 The work is exciting and challenging

New projects get a sense of energy from the feeling that they are being creative and are breaking new ground. Effective projects have an atmosphere around them and a style that is often dynamic, fast and informal. Some risks are allowed.

These features need managing, they do not just happen. They need leadership, organisation and teamwork. Starting a new project is hard work and needs determination to see it through.

It is interesting to note that the issue of finance and available resources is absent from this list: it is not that they are not important, but that they need to be viewed in a proper perspective and considered at the right time. Usually, in a successful project the idea, needs and project vision are developed first and the search for cash and resources comes second. Often, trying to do it the other way round will mean that the project becomes funder-led. All of the ingenuity, ideas and energy behind it are suppressed to ensure that it fits the perceived interests and constraints of possible funders.

Two types of projects

One way of classifying new projects is to divide them into 'supply-side' and 'demand-side' projects.

A supply-side project is one which is developed because resources are available for a particular type of project. Money becomes available (often as a result of underspending at the end of the financial year) and invitations to put forward projects are invited. The lead-time in getting a project up and running has to be fast; usually the project has to be in place by a deadline. Mistakes can be made easily as things are done quickly; in working with supply-side projects, some organisations have had difficulties. Often the project is finance-led, no time is available to test it out or consult with its users, and at times all of the emphasis is about getting the money spent before the end of the financial year. For example, one organisation now keeps several project outlines 'on ice'. Should resources become available, it can adapt the project quickly to fit the relevant criteria.

Demand-side projects are a result of people recognising new or existing needs or gaps in provision. Often someone with a view or a sense of vision is crucial in acting as a catalyst to get people to recognise a need and generate an idea to meet it. Demand-side projects usually take longer to develop; considerable work is needed to explain the project, win support and secure backing for it. Demand-side projects can struggle to get access to funding.

Projects and the sector

The increased use of projects raises several issues and challenges for voluntary agencies. Some of these challenges are not particularly new, but the movement to projects does mean that managers need to think carefully about how their organisation approaches project management and how fixed-term projects can change the nature and operation of their organisation. Some of the key issues for the voluntary sector are outlined below.

Funding becoming project-based

Increasingly, funders and commissioners have moved away from open-ended support to organisations and now prefer to support specific projects rather than to core fund an organisation. Organisations need to develop management and financial systems that show the real cost of the project, including the cost to the organisation of taking it on and managing it.

Funders looking for impact

Funders and commissioners need evidence that the initiatives they fund are delivering and making a difference. The specific and focused nature of a project should make measurement easier; however, one needs to be able to measure both the activity of the project and the longer-term effects and changes that it creates. It is not enough to show that a project is busy.

What comes first: the funding or the need?

Many voluntary organisations have run into problems by chasing whatever funding is available. Organisations can fall into the trap of bidding for projects, not because the project fits with their vision or priorities, but because they need to take on a new project to keep the organisation going. Chasing funding and reinventing an organisation to fit with whatever is currently in vogue can lead to an organisation losing its sense of identity and purpose.

Stop–start–stop

The short-term nature of projects can lead to organisations having to expand rapidly as they take on projects, then scale down as projects come to an end. This can lead to organisational anxiety and stress, as an organisation has to reconfigure itself regularly to deal with changes in its size and range of projects.

Need to think beyond the project

Projects by their nature are usually fixed term. However, most of the issues and user needs that organisations deal with are longer term and cannot be packaged neatly into a two or three-year project timeframe. The project might end, but need and expectation are likely to continue.

Always developing new projects

The increased use of projects means that organisations have to be able to define and win support for new projects. Organisations need to find ways of developing projects that are innovative, challenging and appealing to potential backers, but also realistic and achievable.

In researching this book, five core factors were identified to be useful in helping organisations cope with projects.

1 A clear organisational vision and strategy

Clarity about the organisation's purpose and its immediate direction should ensure that projects fit into the bigger picture. In addition, such clarity should help the organisation to test ideas for new projects, in order to ensure that they fit with the organisation.

2 An organised approach to project management

As organisations become more project-based, they need to develop a consistent and practical approach for designing, planning and managing projects.

3 Flexible structures and ways of working

Organisations need to be able to cope with the need to start up new projects, manage staff on short-term contracts and ensure that the organisation is able to support and develop new projects.

4 Robust costing and planning techniques

In the past, organisations have often undercosted their activities and failed to plan. In order to survive, organisations need to be able to cost projects accurately and fully, and have a planning system to ensure that a project can deliver, and can review and monitor progress.

5 A strong and permanent core

Organisations need an infrastructure or core which can coordinate, organise and oversee projects, and this core needs to be permanent. Its role is more than a management or bureaucratic one; it needs to be able to connect all the organisations and provide quality leadership and support to ensure that projects are effective.

No logical formula

Experience suggests that the life of a project does not follow a logical and tidy path. This book is designed around six main processes and groups of tasks, which usually are not neat and tidy incremental steps, but are inclined to merge. Management of a new project requires coordination of all of the tasks and careful organisation.

Encouraging innovation

There is little point in new projects simply copying what is being done already; it would be easier simply to extend or replicate what is already working rather than go through the work involved in creating a new project. However, new ideas are often rare or discouraged by the way that we work. Innovation and creative thinking can be in short supply, and they need to be encouraged, supported and managed.

Testing the idea

There are several ways of testing out a new idea. Independent studies can be commissioned to research the idea's feasibility and viability. Pilots can be developed. It is also possible simply to run with the project and see if it works.

Building the case for the project

Before a project can be launched other people will need to be involved and feel a part of it. The essential idea and vision behind the project needs communicating and marketing. A network of alliances, backers and supporters needs to be built around the project.

Getting the project going

The project needs to develop a strong sense of momentum to drive it through its start-up. There must be a strong sense of teamwork. One innovator is usually not enough. The project also needs to develop a plan to guide and monitor the start-up.

Designing the project

Projects need to be goal-centred, fast-moving and able to use limited resources flexibly. Much traditional management practice and many organisational systems militate against this. Projects need to find ways of organising that support to enable them to meet their vision rather than constrain it.

Getting the project organised

Detailed decisions about legal structures, finance and staffing will have a profound impact on the project. These issues must be planned and managed in a way that supports and enhances the project's strategy rather than restricting it.

Four factors in a successful project

Successful project management is about connecting four different and sometimes conflicting factors.

A clear need for the project or a problem	The idea or vision behind the project
Opportunity for the project	Capacity of the project to deliver

1 A clear need for the project or a problem

A project works best when the people developing them understand and appreciate the needs and problems that it has to tackle. It is important to evaluate the need or problem properly. What is its root cause? What are the symptoms? What is the scale of it?

2 The idea or vision behind the project

Projects need a vision to unite all of their activities and efforts. It is from the vision that strategies, objectives and workplans flow. The big idea behind the project should be clear enough to show how it will make a significant and sustainable difference to the need or problem.

3 Opportunity for the project

Projects need to have or create the space in which to operate, and need to be supported and backed actively with more than just money. There must be support for the project from key people and a genuine commitment to see it through.

4 Capacity of the project to deliver

Projects need the right balance of skills, energy, resources and organisation to get up and go and deliver results. Projects need to be designed so that they are able to make an impact and create results.

All of these factors need to be looked at and evaluated equally in the design of a project. Too much focus on one or two factors can lead to others being ignored.

Four balancing acts

New project development can be hard. Internal and external factors can easily be stacked against you. Here are four of the main issues with which most new project developers have to juggle.

1 Insecurity and short-term vision

One senior local authority manager commented:

> *Timespans have become shorter. We are under pressure to have things up and running much quicker. We need to see projects delivering much faster. Lead times have been cut. This is partly because we are often under pressure to spend money from central government and other funding programmes before a fixed deadline, and also because our policymakers are increasingly impatient for change and seem to regularly change and alter priorities. For me, long-term planning is about 18 months. I doubt that there are many people who could commit themselves to supporting a project financially for more than one year or two. Long-term and secure funding is unlikely to happen.*

This situation can cause insecurity easily and discourages long-term planning, and it can create a 'hand-to-mouth' existence for projects, living from one grant application to another. Consequently, any long-term vision is lost or shelved.

2 Security versus flexibility

At the start of a new venture it is impossible to be certain of how things will work once it is up and running. What skills will be needed? What will be the pattern of costs and income? What will be the issues that the project will deal with? Therefore, it is logical to resist detailed planning and try to keep things flexible. However, funders often want to see stable and safe projects with detailed workplans and proper control systems. Understandably, staff want secure terms and conditions of employment with a detailed job description. Managing the balance between stability and the need for flexibility and responsiveness is a difficult act in most organisations.

3 Fear of risk and wanting innovative solutions

In the private sector the companies that are committed to new product research and development accept that many new ideas in which they invest time and money will never make it to market. This money will never produce a return on their investment. These companies have learned to live with, and indeed plan for, failure. In the voluntary sector, such a view is rare. Trustees are concerned about their legal responsibility as guardians of charitable money, funders express sharp concerns about wastage, and managers are concerned about their credibility if projects do not succeed. However, the issue of risk and the potential for failure need to be considered if an individual or organisation is to do anything beyond being safe, ordinary and predictable.

4 Balancing planning and doing

No feasibility study, market research report, cost–benefit analysis or external consultancy report will guarantee that a project will work. Often, only doing it can test it properly. Many successful projects were never planned, tested or piloted properly, the people behind them just set them up. They worked hard at ensuring that the project worked. Such talk of bold innovation and social entrepreneurship usually overlooks a host of projects that did not deliver. Project failures are conveniently forgotten. To win resources and manage risk, promoters of new projects increasingly have to demonstrate that their idea is tested properly, is needed and has been designed. You need to decide how much time to put into testing and designing the project, and when to 'grasp the nettle' and launch it.

Three different perspectives on projects

I am starting to get worried. Sure, our estate has got major problems, but I am getting fed up with all these well-intentioned projects that keep turning up and then disappearing. Some organisations seem to be able to grab whatever funding is going, parachute into an area, make all sorts of promises about what they are going to do, and then just at the point when people are starting to use and rely upon them, they close down as the funding has ran out. Sometimes I wonder why they bothered!

Volunteer secretary, community association

I have noticed a familiar pattern in three-year projects. In the first year, a worker is appointed, who then has to spend most of the year trying to find out what it is that they are supposed to be doing. This usually involves trying to reconcile what is actually wanted and needed with whatever was in the original funding bid.

In the second year things start to happen. The work starts to appear, people get involved and expectations rise.

In the third and final year, project workers start worrying about their future employment. Some might leave before the end. Demoralisation sets in. The project either ends suddenly or it fades out. This can't be a sensible way to organise things.

Finance manager, medium-sized voluntary organisation

The trustees of our foundation are clear that we want to be an innovative funder. We do not see it as our role to fund things on a permanent basis – that should usually be the job of government. Our role is to pump-prime things, demonstrate practice and 'give wings' to new ideas. That's why we encourage organisations to develop realistic projects.

Secretary, charitable foundation

About project management

Organisations often approach projects in an unplanned and *ad hoc* way. An application is made for funding, based on a rough idea for a project or on what the organisation thinks that the funder will back. The funding is agreed, and then there is a sense of urgency to appoint staff, get organised and get the project up and running before the deadline.

A worker in a health agency described how projects were approached in her organisation:

> *Sometimes we get bounced into running a project. There is little time given at the start to any detailed objective setting or planning – all the work goes into the funding bid. If the bid is successful, we are inclined to throw the project together. Project workers are given a blank sheet of paper and told to get on with it. Core staff are asked to get involved in the project alongside their day job. It's a mess. When a project does work, it is usually despite the organisation!*

A project framework

This chapter introduces a framework for managing projects. The framework is drawn from ideas and concepts which have influenced the development of project management as a specific discipline or branch of management thinking. This approach aims to tackle some specific features of managing projects.

Projects need clear lines of accountability

Various players have an investment or an interest in a project – some might have put the money up for it, others might have backed it in other ways. The project might affect the work of other people.

Projects need to involve people

Few projects are a one-man or one-woman show. Projects need to draw people in, get cooperation and work with and through other people.

Projects are about delivery

Projects are expected to deliver. Often there are high expectations. They need to get on with it and not be a 'talking shop'. Projects needs structures that are simple and flexible, and support rather than hinder their work.

A model framework

This framework has been developed from those used in different organisations.

The project sponsor is the agency that approves the project and allocates the resources for it. Their role might be an active sponsoring one: the project might be their idea, they might have written the brief and commissioned the delivery of the project, or their role might just be a simple funding one, where they have chosen to back a bid to run a project. In larger organisations there might be an internal sponsor, such as the chief executive or a management board. An external sponsor is often a funder.

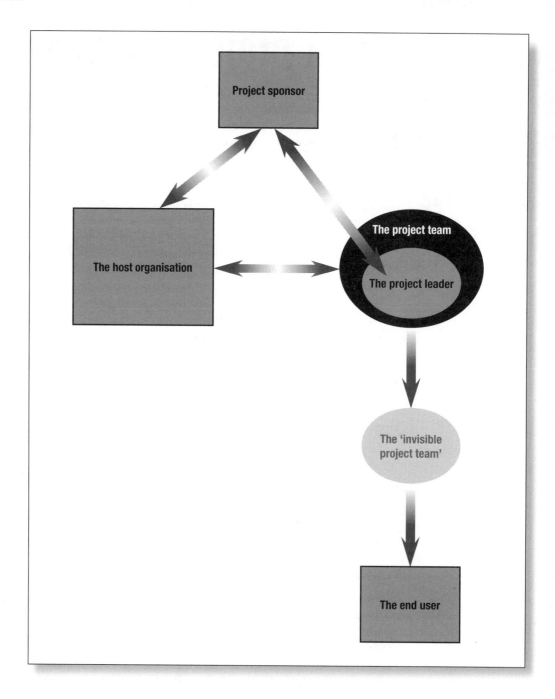

The host organisation is usually a permanent body which has taken the decision to manage the project. The project might be an integral part of the host agency's work or the host agency's role might be a more detached one of providing a base for the project. The host agency is responsible for managing the project and being accountable for its resources and performance. Often the host organisation has a key role in managing the relationship between the project and the project sponsor, where the host has to report to the sponsor on the project's performance, and the host is usually the accountable body. In addition, the host can play a valuable role in smoothing out and resolving any problems that might occur in the relationship.

The project leader is the individual responsible for delivering the project. The project leader might be recruited and employed just to work on the project – when the project ends, their contract ends – or they might be a worker in the host agency who is seconded to work on the project alongside their other duties. In addition, there may be a project team made up of people who will work with the project leader to deliver the project.

The invisible project team is an interesting concept. In their work on project management, writers Briner, Geddes and Hastings (1996) use the concept of the invisible project team to describe this role. These are the people with whom the project needs to work to be successful: their support, goodwill and commitment will be crucial to the project's long-term success:

- potential partners
- early or pilot users
- representatives
- opinion formers
- gatekeepers
- resource controllers
- people who will carry on the work after the project.

The end-users are the individuals or groups who should benefit from the project: they might be identifiable individuals or communities. Often, contact with the end-user comes through the invisible project team, and in this model, several potential conflicts or tensions need to be managed.

The sponsor and the user

An interesting issue can be about what the sponsor thinks is needed and wanted and what the intended users actually need and want. Solutions to misunderstood problems can be delivered from on high but fail because no one has bothered to find out what is really needed. Often the sponsor is driven by the need to deliver targets or spend money, or has an outdated view of what is needed. A key role for the project leader is to resolve this issue, and not to assume that because the sponsor has decided to back something, it will work.

The host and the project

Although the project is a temporary part of the host organisation it needs to have a level of independence to operate. The project needs an identity and focus, but this should fit with that of the host organisation, as it is the host that carries the responsibilities and risks. The host organisation needs to be properly and fairly paid for the work involved in taking the project on and supporting it. It is very easy for a host to have to subsidise an undercosted project: resources and people's time can leak from the host to the project. Conversely, in some instances hosts cream off a project management fee and do very little for it. A useful approach is to draw up an agreement between the host and the project, setting out the roles of the project and the host and arrangements for managing resources.

To whom is the project leader accountable?

Project working can lead to confusing working relationships. One project manager described how he felt that he had several bosses:

> My line manager, the project sponsor, the project steering group and key users all have very strong opinions about what I and the project should be doing – sometimes I feel that I am being pulled in several different directions at once.

Therefore, it is important that the definition of what the project is about and the project plan are clearly agreed and documented and that lines of accountability are simple.

The role of the sponsor

Being the sponsor is more than just agreeing to fund the project: it should and can be a really valuable role. It needs a strategic view – an ability to see the bigger picture, not to get lost in the operational details. Here are some useful roles that a sponsor can play.

Role	Activities
To get or allocate the resources to the project.	The sponsor might be the agency that holds the funds or manages the funds on behalf of another.
To give the go-ahead to the project.	The sponsor will approve the project and commission it.
To approve the project definition.	There needs to be a process of negotiation and influence as to what the project's intended outcomes and outputs should be.
To approve the overall project plan.	The sponsor will sign off the project's plan.
To be involved in monitoring the project.	The sponsor will receive regular monitoring reports showing how the project's operation compares with its plan.
To give authority to the project.	The sponsor lends its name and credibility to the project by backing it.
To contribute to the project's exit strategy.	The sponsor should have an interest in what happens to the project in the longer term.
To take part in the project evaluation.	The sponsor should be involved actively in the evaluation to review what difference it has made and to identify learning for the future.

The sponsor's role is very much a strategic one. It is not the sponsor's role to manage the project directly or be involved in its day-to-day work; often it is the sponsor who has had the idea for the project and commissioned the host organisation to deliver it. Usually, the sponsor will make the decision to back the project and allocate or find the resources to back it. The sponsor needs to have sufficient status and influence to provide support for the project. Sponsors must feel comfortable with delegation. They should be able to set the direction, agree the project definition and then let the project get on with it. It is the role of the sponsor to steer, but not to row.

The role of the host

The host is the organisation that houses the project. It can play several roles.

Role	Activities
Incubator	To provide practical support and expertise to nurture the project and enable it to move from an idea into a project.
Organisational support	To provide office space, administrative support and access to resources. This should make the project start-up more economical as it can pay for shared resources rather than have to buy its own.
An accountable structure	The project is allowed to operate under the host's name rather than becoming a separate organisation.
Credibility	The project benefits from its reputation and brand by using the host's name to attract support.
Marketing or networking	The project uses the host's network of contacts to develop its work.

At one level it has a very practical role in providing or organising the physical space for the project, being the legal employer of project staff and providing administrative and organisational support to the project. The project is a temporary part of the host organisation, so usually the host is legally responsible for the project. Often, it is the host which had the idea for the project, developed that idea and secured the resources for the project from the sponsor. It is important that the project fits with the host organistion's strategic priorities and ethos. A good host organisation can help the project to deliver by allowing the project to use its contacts, networks and reputation.

Role of the project leader

Here are some key roles that a project leader can play.

Role	Activities
To ensure that the project is properly defined.	The project leader needs to ensure that there is an active agreement as to what the project is meant to achieve, and that all elements of the project's success criteria are defined and agreed.
To cost and plan the project.	Costing and preparing a project plan and detailed budget should fall within the project leader's role, as they will have responsibility for managing these.
To design how the project is going to work.	The project leader should have sufficient technical or subject knowledge in order to work out how the project can best meet its objectives.
To lead, develop and organise any project team.	If there is a project team, the project leader will have a key role in helping it to develop, leading team meetings and helping individual team members to contribute.
To keep the project's stakeholders in touch with the project.	The project leader will need to communicate, use networks and build up personal contacts to ensure that the sponsor, key users and others are informed about the project and are 'wired in'.
Controlling the project's resources.	The project leader should have delegated levels of responsibility for controlling the budget and other resources allocated to the project.
To prepare, collate and explain project monitoring information.	The project leader will need to organise the production of regular monitoring information to ensure that the project can be monitored and held accountable. The project leader should have responsibility for presenting the information and helping people to understand it.
To lead delivery of the project.	Most of the project leader's time will be focused on delivery – ensuring that users get the intended services or activities. They need to be skilled in operational management.
To implement and work on the project's exit strategy.	The project leader should have responsibility for ensuring that the project's exit strategy (that is, what happens after the project) is worked on and developed.
To contribute to evaluation of the project.	The project leader should have a key role in contributing to the project's evaluation. Experience would suggest that the leader is not the best person to do the evaluation as they often lack objectivity or are too close to the project, but they need to be a key player in the evaluation process.

The project leader or manager is the individual responsible for delivering the project. They may work on the project full time or the management of the project might be one of the tasks that is added to their day-to-day role. The project leader's role is a mix of organisational, managerial and political skills. They must accept responsibility for ensuring that the project happens and meets the objectives established for it in the definition stage.

A project leader needs a range of skills. They will be responsible for the project's detailed design and implementation. They also have a key role in bringing other people into the project and keeping stakeholders in touch and on-board.

Some project leaders are recruited to work exclusively on the project. They work on it full-time and, when the project ends, their employment also ends. In some cases a project team is established. The team needs to be task-orientated and led in such as way as to be able to support the project leader in delivering the project, rather than becoming another meeting for the project leader to service.

The 'project from hell'

Here are 10 tried-and-tested ways to ruin a voluntary sector project.

1 **Grab whatever funding is going**
'All funding is good. We'll do whatever the funders want, provided there is money in it! We will reinvent ourselves and take on projects to do whatever is the flavour of the month.'

2 **See planning as a luxury**
'There is no point spending time writing plans, as things will just turn up.'

3 **Do not bother to check what is actually wanted or needed**
'We have been in this sector for years, so there is little that we can learn from the people whom the project is supposed to benefit. Their needs or aspirations rarely change.'

4 **Load responsibility for the project on to one person**
'In the name of "empowerment" we appoint or pick someone as project leader and expect them to be accountable for the entire project. We expect them to be a Jack or Jill of all trades.'

5 **Do it on the cheap: undercost it**
'There is no point asking for the full cost, as we will never get it. Anyway, we are good at scrimping and bodging.'

6 **Store up problems**
'Of course there will be difficulties and things might not be as we expected, but we will battle on and tell everyone that it is just fine.'

7 **Work in splendid isolation**
'Working with people who are doing similar things for the same people can just lead to confusion and competition.'

8 **Create a huge structure to oversee the project**
'Of course, our one worker project needs a steering group, finance subgroup, advisory panel and user group to help them along. It gives them something to do.'

9 **Ignore the future**
'Strategic plan, exit strategies and forward thinking sound great in theory, but we prefer to make the service indispensible so that the funders will feel morally obliged to refund it.'

10 **Do not learn: get on to the next project**
'Evaluation sounds great in theory, but we are too busy getting ready for our next project to learn any lessons from past ones.'

On being a project sponsor

An experienced project sponsor described their experience:

In my role as a manager in an NHS organisation I am probably involved in sponsoring around 10 projects delivered by external agencies at any one time. It's a role that I have had very little direction in and I, like most of my colleagues, have had no formal training in [commissioning or sponsoring projects].

Over the years we have made several mistakes. I have got too involved in the day-to-day operations of some projects to the point of almost becoming a senior project leader. In others I have assumed that the project workers have the same understanding of what is needed and intended as I have. At times, I think I have failed to explain to people that I work in an organisation that can be very risk-averse and expects me to know what is going on, which is why I have to keep asking for information.

A good project sponsor needs to do the following things.

Stay focused on the bigger picture

It is easy to get lost in the detail. It is much better to keep asking about the outcomes rather than what the project is doing. It is the sponsor's job to make sure that the users and the community get something that makes a positive difference. The precise detail and the means used to reach that end is up to the project leader.

Be specific about what is needed

Often, ideas for projects are 'half-baked'. Someone has found a pot of money and needs it to be spent, the need is never researched properly and the definition stage is rushed. The project's aims are vague or meaningless. It is the sponsor's role to make sure that a project's definition is clear and comprehensive. Part of this is making sure that any hidden agendas are brought to the surface. If time is not spent in the definition stage, the project is likely to run into problems later.

Open doors for the project

Sometimes the sponsor can act as a champion or ambassador for a project. They can use their networks and contacts to introduce the project and build its profile.

Focus on the future

Increasingly, the sponsor needs to be thinking about what happens after the project: what is the point of doing a project if it does not make a lasting difference? The sponsor needs to be involved in discussions about exit strategies and how the project can be taken forward.

Over the past 10 years we must have housed something like 20 or so different projects. Often they come about because a group of people have an idea, but do not want the hassle of creating a new and independent legal structure to run what might be a relatively short-term project, so they prefer to operate it under our umbrella. In other cases, our development team often starts something off as a pilot with a view to it leaving us and becoming an independent venture.

Usually, these arrangements work well, but we have had some problems. Often we end up subsidising the project and find that staff time and admin resources are inclined to leak into propping up projects. Sometimes, project budgets have not included an adequate amount to cover our management costs. On one occasion we got involved in managing a project that was way beyond our competency, and possibly our legal powers. It is as if all the risk is with us.

In recent years we have become much better at how we house projects. Our trustees have developed a checklist that they use before starting out on any project. We also ask people involved to sign up to a document that makes it clear that we have legal responsibilities for things like employment of staff and accountability of funds. We have also started a process of reviewing all projects on a six-monthly basis to see if they should stay with us or work towards independence.

Director, local development agency

The key stages of a project

Stage	Key tasks	Key issues	Your issues
Defining and testing	■ Turning an idea or an opportunity into a project ■ Agreeing outcomes of what the project should do, change or prevent ■ Checking that the project is feasible.	■ Need to ensure that the project is thought through fully and that various stakeholders are actively involved ■ A danger that the project is partly defined: 'Spend the budget by April.'	
Gaining and support	■ Communicating the idea behind the project ■ Getting funders and commissioners to support it ■ Involving people in developing the idea.	■ Need to develop a clear and concise way of pitching the project to win backing and support.	
Defining and planning	■ Deciding on the structure of the project ■ Working out the full cost of the project ■ Building a team approach.	■ Fully costing the project ■ Working out the best kind of structure needed to deliver the project ■ Developing a realistic and flexible project plan.	
Rolling it out	■ Launching the project ■ Building momentum ■ Sustaining the work ■ Keeping it on track.	■ Getting other people involved ■ Ensuring that the project does not drift ■ Monitoring progress ■ Communicating.	
Closing the project	■ Implementing an exit strategy ■ Ensuring that the project's outcomes will be sustained and carried forward ■ Managing the closure.	■ Focusing on the end ■ Making sure that the project's work will continue ■ Bringing things to a conclusion.	
Project evaluation	■ Being able to show what the project has done ■ Learning from the project's experience ■ Recording and disseminating the learning.	■ Being accountable, demonstrating that the project has delivered ■ Learning from what has and has not worked ■ Ensuring that the project's experience is fed into other activities and future projects.	

3

Turning an idea into a project

This chapter looks at the process of developing ideas for projects, how organisations can encourage and discourage innovation, and how to test the feasibility of an idea. Ideas for projects come from different sources. Some are the result of identifying unmet or changing needs; others come from someone having an idea or a vision of what they want to achieve. Some come from an opportunity emerging, such as a new funding source opening up. In many respects the ability of organisations to develop ideas, be innovative and test out their feasibility is what keeps them vibrant and alive.

A truly innovative idea or project sounds like a exclusive, once-in-a-lifetime event which can be dreamed up only by talented individuals with exceptional intelligence, creativity and imagination. In reality, few organisations would want seriously to manage the process of having and developing ideas in such an idealistic way. There is little direct research into how voluntary or public sector organisations develop new services or activities, even though it seems almost mandatory to claim in annual reports, funding bids and publicity material that all work is always innovative and groundbreaking.

Creative innovation

There are very few original ideas. Most successful innovations are the successful adaptation of an existing idea or the connecting together of a problem and a solution. Innovations are rarely big or huge initiatives; usually they build on what is already happening.

Many ideas happen accidentally or in the wrong place. One study by Jewkes et al., in their book *The Sources of Invention* (1969), found that of 57% of major inventions, ranging from ballpoint pens to engineering techniques, 48% were discovered while looking for something else or were invented by people who should have been doing something else with their time at work.

Often, innovations happen despite the official management and decision-making systems in the organisation; they occur in the shadows of the organisation.

CASE STUDY

One established project working with ex-offenders developed a new and successful system of peer support and groupwork without ever talking to anyone at the organisation's headquarters. Four years later, the scheme now employs three staff and has an expanding network of volunteers. The project leader described the process of innovation that they adopted:

We knew that if we asked for permission to introduce the new support system it would take ages. Papers would have to be written, reports commissioned and studies done. It would have left our hands and been taken over. Instead, we went ahead with it and quietly started piloting it. Once we knew that it was working, we then introduced it to our senior managers in order to secure new funds for it. To their credit, they supported it.

Many new projects are started more by chance than by organised planning. The management writer Henry Mintzberg (1994) makes an interesting distinction between deliberate and emergent strategy in organisations. A deliberate strategy is when managers clearly set out to plan how they want their organisation to develop. An emergent strategy is when things happen as a result of chance, opportunity and even accident. Many organisations have invested heavily in commissioning research, designing blueprints and detailed budgeting only to find that their best laid plans are out of date as soon as the ink is dry. Deliberate strategy is necessary: without it, total chaos would reign. However, too much deliberate strategy can make an organisation very unresponsive and inflexible.

Deliberate strategy comes from:

- formal plans
- the budget
- workplans
- external contracts

Emergent strategy comes from:

- chance and accidents
- people's pet projects
- having the time to do something different
- trying things out and commitments

A director of an arts centre described how she struggles to manage the relationship between these two elements.

By the nature of our work people are having ideas all the time. Several of our workers are very capable of getting involved in something by chance or working on what interests them. On balance it pays off, but it can be a bit chaotic. Most of our established and successful activities started out as a pet project of one or two staff. If they want the idea to become a project they have to get backing for it. They have to navigate it into the formal side of the centre. They have to get a budget for it, get it programmed into our plans and get staff time to work on it. My job is to ensure a balance between the deliberate parts of the organisation (budgets, workplan, resources, business plans and contract obligations) and the emergent or chance activities.

Types of innovation

It is possible to identify three types of innovation.

1 A new activity, service or product

Finding a new way of meeting a need is a typical innovation. The voluntary sector has a track record in creating, sponsoring and setting up new projects to meet new needs. Community transport schemes, citizens' advice bureaux and community businesses are all examples of initiatives put together to meet a need.

2 A new development in practice

Many new innovations are concerned with developing different or improved ways of managing an existing problem or activity. This can include developing new processes or new techniques or using new technology.

3 A new strategy, direction or approach

A different type of innovation is the creation of an entirely different vision, values and direction for an organisation. Examples could include changing the whole basis of how an organisation works by giving greater control to users, or by changing fundamentally the type of work. Sometimes this only can be achieved by creating a new organisation or distinct project.

The process of innovation

Creating an atmosphere that encourages new thinking

Fresh from an intensive (and expensive) residential management course, the director of a housing association called in his staff. He told them that they had his full support to think creatively, take risks and be innovative. After his pep talk, experienced members of staff remembered their last experience of innovation. A new project had failed to live up to original expectations. Despite considerable effort and commitment from the project leader, the results had been mixed and disappointing. The association had reacted by reducing the project's resources, gradually closing it down and reallocating the project leader to a boring and mundane job. The project leader was a talented and intelligent individual who had thought it was understood that some risk was involved. He was now regarded as a failure. The association gave out a mixed message: 'Be creative and innovative' was the public slogan, but the hidden text was 'But whatever you do … don't ever get anything less than 100% right.'

Creating an atmosphere that encourages people to question the status quo, look for better ways of doing things and come up with new ideas is not easy. A critical issue is stressing the importance of learning as a central feature of organisational life. Good learning creates an openness, inquisitiveness and curiosity which may lead to new insights and ideas. Several organisations are trying to develop the idea of a learning company which sees learning not just in a narrow sense, such as attending external courses or job-related training, but also encouraging curiosity and long-term development and change. Learning is seen as a main building block of the organisation.

The following ideas are examples of how it is possible to create an atmosphere that encourages fresh thinking and innovation.

Encourage learning

Creating an organisation which encourages learning as a continuous activity can lead to many new ideas. Learning does not just occur on training courses or in seminars. Effective learning within the workplace can be organised in many ways: mentors, secondments, distance learning, coaching and guided reading are all examples. For example, a housing association is experimenting with the idea of giving each member of staff a minimum of five days' learning entitlement per year. They can use this time to attend formal courses, but many are using it to evaluate existing services and develop ideas for new ones.

Encourage evaluation

Building in regular evaluation activities can be a way to encourage new ideas. Evaluation techniques include surveys, review meetings, audits and discussion groups. For example, an arts centre now holds a review conference after each event, which has two parts: a 'post mortem' discussion, looking at what worked and what did not; and a 'what next' session to look at what has been learned and to generate ideas for the future.

Encourage curiosity

Often in organisations, working practices and processes fall into a routine. Things happen because they have always happened. The budget and the workplan are based on what happened last year, and the organisation operates on 'automatic pilot'. Encouraging people to ask why they do things is important and can be challenging. Getting an organisation focused on the results and impact of its work rather than its volume can be one way of encouraging fresh thinking.

Encourage feedback

Developing new means of generating comments, reactions and complaints from the organisation's users, staff and other contacts can lead to several insights. Formal systems such as complaint procedures, satisfaction and review sheets are part of the process but are no substitute for 'walking the job': i.e. walking around the office and observing and listening to people. Even negative feedback such as a complaint can highlight the way in which an activity can be improved, changed or enhanced.

Encourage flexibility

People need to see the wider context and effect of what they are doing: jobs and work can be compartmentalised and few people see the whole picture. Through flexible working, job shadowing and job enlargement people see much more of the whole picture. For example, an architect's practice changed how it managed projects. Staff were encouraged to manage a project through from start to finish and to visit it regularly after its handover. This small change (often called job enlargement) led to several improvements and better coordination of projects.

Encourage movement

Often, people become stuck in a particular job. Their perspective of, and involvement in, their work becomes narrow and they lose a sense of vision and purpose. Some organisations are encouraging staff to move around different projects, become multi-skilled and use appraisals and review meetings to chart their progress. Well planned and supported movements can help to encourage an exchange of ideas and views. Developing teamwork, encouraging people to think outside of their usual scope and helping people to see the whole picture can help to bring in new perspectives.

Manage conflict

Conflict can be seen as wholly negative and to be discouraged at all costs; however, well-managed conflict, which is focused on the problem and not the personalities involved, can spark off many insights and ideas. Getting different parties to a conflict to work together to define the issue, explore root causes and generate possible ways forward could provide new and valuable ideas.

Experiment with structures

New ways of working such as secondments, project or task groups and teamwork can lead to creative solutions. The structures should help people to look at things from a different viewpoint and develop new ideas.

CASE STUDY

A national development agency has used project teams extensively over the past two years to develop key projects. Four or five staff from different functions work together for a short period on an issue and come up with a plan. Often the people with the least prior experience of the issue make the most valuable contribution: asking apparently obvious questions challenges conventional practice and assumptions.

Get away from it all

It is possible to be too close to a problem to think about it creatively. For example, one company found that staff returning after short breaks, sabbaticals or transfers came back with a different insight to a long-term problem. Another organisation – a charity for people with learning difficulties – holds an annual 'ideas day'. All staff, board members and volunteers meet off-site and must bring at least three new ideas on which to work. The day works through each idea and develops a shortlist of ideas to implement on return.

Borrow from others

Some organisations have got the process of 'stealing' from others down to a fine art. Keeping in touch with developments in your field through professional bodies, networks and conferences is important. One project organises what it calls 'raiding parties', where staff visit similar organisations to look at how they do things and see what could be adapted in their project.

Look at what you do not do

When she had to cover for the centre's receptionist, the manager of a training agency realised that the organisation overlooked a valuable source of ideas. A fair proportion of calls to the agency were from local people and other agencies enquiring about things that the organisation did not provide or offer. These calls were answered politely with the response: 'Sorry, we don't do that ... goodbye.' The manager realised that these calls were a valuable source of ideas. They represented unmet need, but the centre did not record or use them. The centre has now adopted a simple procedure for recording requests that are turned down. Analysis of this information has led to several ideas for new services and projects.

Exploring possible sources of new ideas

New ideas can be developed in many different places. Here are four ways in which new ideas can be discovered.

1 A fresh look at what you are doing already

This can happen either through formal processes such as commissioning an evaluation of what you do, carrying out surveys or comparing your organisation with others in the same field. It can also happen accidentally.

One environmental agency developed an entirely new way of working with schoolchildren as a result of some challenging questions asked by a newly-appointed clerical worker. She thought that the way the schools programme was organised was out-of-date and unimaginative. After asking several awkward but painfully obvious questions, she persuaded the rest of the team to work with her to develop a new and very different project.

2 Challenging the way that you look at a problem

Often we get stuck into a predictable and routine way of thinking about a problem. We do not challenge or rethink our assumptions about it or ever look at the difference between the problem's root causes and symptoms. Trying to see an issue from a different perspective, thinking laterally rather than just logically, or testing the validity of assumptions about the problem can lead to a creative solution. We can jump to solutions without checking first that we fully appreciate the problem and all of its aspects.

CASE STUDY

A voluntary agency had debated for years what to do with its overcrowded and increasingly expensive city centre office. Various solutions were debated, such as moving, changing the office layout and building an extension. A session on creative thinking led to a different solution. At least half of the staff were supposed to be working on neighbourhood projects and did not need to be office-based. The office was only ever overcrowded between 10am and 4pm, and it was particularly overcrowded when field staff had to attend meetings, use the computers and attend supervision sessions. The agreed solution was that the central office needed to be smaller, with two satellite sub-bases rented near to where the neighbourhood workers worked. Meetings and supervision sessions would be held at the sub-bases. Field workers would be given laptop computers to enable emailing material to and from the main office. This solution created significant benefits. It reduced travel costs, reduced stress at the central office and, most importantly, refocused the organisation by shifting the physical presence to the local neighbourhoods from the city centre. By looking at the problem differently, it discovered a useful and fruitful solution.

3 Adapting a solution from elsewhere to a new problem

Many innovations occur when something can be adapted from one use to another: all it requires is the capacity to make a connection between a need and a link to a possible solution elsewhere. Much of the technology we use in our households started out life in industrial, commercial or specialist fields. For example, the TV remote control was designed originally as a niche specialist product for people with disabilities; it was not seen as having much mainstream potential.

4 Following up an opportunity

Many established organisations lack the capacity to identify new needs and encourage feedback from users; they are inward-looking and operate to a very narrow menu of what they can provide and offer. A severe example of this was the manager of a local authority service, who complained that members of the public kept phoning up his staff and 'asking for the wrong things'. Some organisations define themselves so tightly that opportunities are dismissed as irrelevant. People working in a particular sector or field make sense of this by developing their own language, practice and style. This is understandable, but can lead to a very narrow focus which can relate only to people who speak the same language. Narrow thinking leads to a compartmental approach to thinking. Our starting point is what we do now, not what is needed. Creative thinking requires us to move away from our usual way of looking at or describing something.

We need to learn and innovate from what we already do. We need to develop a broader understanding of what is happening in the world outside and be willing to be flexible as to how we can respond. Opportunities are missed as people are too busy dealing with day-to-day issues.

Most organisations do what they are doing now as a result of history. They are driven by what they did last year. Often, to keep going and ensure that existing expectations and commitments are met is enough; the internal routine takes over. The main driving force is survival and ensuring that things continue from one month to another. The organisation develops an atmosphere in which it is too busy to think, plan and respond to new opportunities.

Managing innovation within the organisation

Managing an organisation that genuinely supports and encourages innovation is hard: it involves undoing a whole way of operating and managing which has developed over time, but for innovation to happen within an organisation, this process is necessary. The alternative is for managers to pay lip service to creating new activities, but to become frustrated as little happens.

Project development cycle time

In certain industries (in particular the car and computer industries) considerable effort has been made to cut down the time that it takes to develop, design and produce a new product. The time involved in product development is known as the 'time to market'. New models of cars can be designed, tested, engineered and produced in three to four years, as opposed to the seven years it used to take. Many companies believe that their competitive edge will come increasingly from being first to the market with new and innovative products and services.

Organisations have invested heavily in streamlining new product development systems, creating much more effective internal processes and rewarding successful individuals and teams. Few not-for-profit agencies have the resources available to invest internally or reward success in financial terms. However, it is interesting to look at what (if any) internal process manages the development of new projects.

CASE STUDY

In one well-established organisation a brief review was carried out. This was prompted by the comments of one individual that 'it took so long to get an idea agreed that it was not worth bothering with, as by the time approval was given it would be too late'. Three projects were used as case studies. Development time (the time from having the idea to the project being launched) ranged from nine months for a media campaign to three years for a local project. Despite innovation being one of the main buzzwords of its new mission statement, very little actually happened. New ideas had to run an obstacle course of meetings, reviews, planning sessions, budget cycles and detailed considerations. Many ideas got lost on the way. If an idea did get through, it was a wonder that there was anything left in it at the end of the process.

In the case study above, the review indicated four problems which frustrated new developments and suggested how they could be tackled.

1 No time

The organisation operated at full capacity. Few individuals had time to think and discuss new ideas, and the working style was all about being seen to be busy.

Action: responsibility for developing new ideas would have to be seen as an explicit part of managing the organisation. Workplans, job descriptions, budgets and meeting agendas should have 'development' built into them.

2 No process

People sponsoring a new idea had to navigate it through a plethora of meetings and committees. Often, responsibility for making a decision to back an idea was avoided or put off: 'New ideas often hung around waiting for a green light.'

Action: responsibility for managing the process of project development and approval should be given to a senior person within the agency. The number of stages involved in getting project approval should be cut.

3 The present comes first

Many people assumed that there was never any money for new ideas – so why bother having them? The main planning activity in the organisation was the annual budget. This should be the clearest statement of priorities. The starting point for putting the budget together was to cost in expenditure for current activities and projects, as there was hardly ever any surplus income to use on new work, and many of the items in the budget were no longer priorities; they were there because of past decisions rather than current strategy.

Action: the organisation should review all of its activities and projects periodically and see how they fit with current direction and needs. Budgets for new projects should be considered at the same time as existing projects and activities.

4 No resources

The organisation did not have any financial resources to invest in new projects. Funders were perceived to be unwilling to allow the organisation to develop any reserves.

Action: the organisation should build up a development fund equivalent to four per cent of its revenue. This fund should be used to support, test and 'pump-prime' new projects. The rationale behind this fund should be argued for in the business plan as a sound management idea.

Owing to structured processes and ways of working, larger organisations can find doing new things much harder than smaller ones. In the private sector, large conglomerates have redesigned themselves into smaller units and have encouraged decentralisation and taskforces to get away from the notion that intelligent thinking and effective management are only the province of corporate headquarters. New ideas can get lost in office politics, demarcation battles and numerous committees and meetings.

One senior manager in a large national charity described how he is trying to turn the organisation around:

> We are working hard to break down the barriers between our head office and local projects. We are reducing the number of things that need to come to us for approval, we are encouraging our project leaders to keep some time back for exploring local needs and planning new projects. We have created a small development budget to work on new ideas or to allow for staff cover to do project development work. We want to turn around the view that all ideas must come from the top. It has not been easy, and will take a while to work properly.

Organisational structures and practices can easily, but unintentionally, discourage people from having or taking forward new ideas. Many organisations operate at or even beyond full capacity. Every hour is in demand and all income is allocated tightly to existing commitments. Most of the structures and practices are about controlling what is happening already rather than allowing space to develop new projects. Tight job descriptions mark off boundaries and sometimes can stop people from seeing the whole picture. Narrowly written funding contracts and business plans mean that every ounce of resource is committed to existing projects and service delivery. The starting point for budget process in most organisations is carrying on last year's commitments and rarely creating any space for new projects. A lack of any uncommitted money or working capital means that opportunities to develop new and worthwhile activities are missed.

Lost opportunities

There is an accounting term called 'opportunity cost', which is when an organisation has committed itself so much, or is using all its existing resources, to the extent that it is unable to follow up or invest in a new opportunity that emerges.

An opportunity cost happens when one decision or activity stops you from being able to do or follow up something else. For example, a contract with a local authority might be so demanding that it leaves you with no time to develop other projects, make contact with other purchasers or bid for other work. The opportunity cost of the local authority contract is the cost that you forgo by not having the management time to develop other work and create other income.

Often we incur opportunity costs by being too busy and not having any uncommitted time or money to explore and test new ideas. A director of a voluntary agency described how he does this:

I have a rule that I spend at least one day a month away from the agency, at conferences, visits to similar projects or with our main user groups. We are a well-established and generally successful organisation, but I get concerned about being complacent and failing to develop. I push people to keep in touch with the outside world. It encourages us to question what we do and helps us to identify options and opportunities for development.

Four factors are useful in the process of deciding to progress a new idea.

1 Focus the discussion on the big picture

The discussion should be on the need for the project, its possible benefits and how it could work. Factors such as detailed costings, who will fund it and staff it are probably unknown at this stage and should not dominate the discussion.

2 Stress the vision

Spend time on why the project is needed. Do not assume that people understand the context, specific situation and need for a new initiative. Often, people presenting a new project have laboured on it for so long or are so enthusiastic about it that they fail to outline the need for it and its background.

3 Acknowledge uncertainties and unknown details

Introducing an idea at this stage can disarm potential objections by drawing attention to things that need testing or further consideration. In addition, it is useful to indicate the possible risks rather than allow people to spot them. They should seek agreement to consider it further and not seek a complete agreement for immediate implementation.

4 Actively seek allies

A new project needs backing early on: a useful way of doing this is to listen to and acknowledge other people's ideas, reactions and suggestions. The project may well fail if it seen as being an individual's pet project or hobby horse. Use people as sounding boards and ask them to add to your idea rather than find fault with it.

Testing the idea

Once you have decided that you have an idea that is worth pursuing, there are three ways forward.

1   You could carry out a feasibility study to check that there is a need for the project, and to check that the project will be able to make an impact on the need.

2   You could pilot the project on a smaller scale for a fixed time to see if it works.

3   You could choose to skip feasibility studies and pilot projects and simply go ahead and do it.

The third choice may seem reckless and extreme. However, it is worth remembering that many effective projects and ideas probably would have failed a feasibility study.

When to skip a feasibility study

- **When time is short.**
  Delaying the project while you do a feasibility study will only lose time. It is more important to do something rather than wait.
- **When you can live with it failing.**
- **When you have sufficient confidence and security to live with failure if it goes wrong.**
  You are able to cope with the risks involved in the project failing.
- **When you can minimise risk.**
  The project is designed to be flexible enough so that it can adapt itself to what works and stop what does not work. It must be able to change course or be able to be closed down painlessly if clearly it is not working. In some projects there is often a point where you can bail out and do something different if it is obvious that the project is not working as assumed. In others, such as large capital projects, usually such bail-out points do not exist.

Making the decision on how to test your idea will be determined by a number of factors:

- the likely attitude of potential funders for the project
- your attitude to risk
- the time and other resources available to test the idea.

It is alleged that scientists at Farnborough carried out a laboratory research exercise into the aerodynamics of the bumblebee and concluded that it would never be able to fly. In many ways, the only true test of whether a project will work is to try it out. Feasibility tests, pilot projects and market research are important, but cannot guarantee success or failure.

The factors that make a successful project are varied. They include many human and one-off factors such as goodwill, luck and local circumstances. Many feasibility studies can be criticised for dealing only with objective information in an illogical world. There is a tendency to consider hard facts and ignore information such as reactions, opinions and comments, which need more interpretation.

However, in order to overcome waste, convince funders and check on the original plans, ideas for projects require some kind of study to show that the idea is sound and worthy of investment. Increasingly, clear evidence is needed to show that a new project could deliver results, is needed and is worth the investment.

What to test?

There are several aspects to feasibility.

- **Financial or business feasibility**
  Is it likely that the project can be delivered and designed within a reasonable budget? Is the project one which either funders will fund, commissioners will contract for or consumers will buy? How viable or tested is the project?
- **Political feasibility**
  Is the project likely to attract support from decision-makers and key influencers? Does the project fit within the organisation's culture and strategy? Could the project damage the organisation's reputation or links with others?
- **Legal feasibility**
  Can the organisation and project comply with all relevant laws and rules?

- **Performance and results feasibility**
  Can the project deliver? Will it really make a difference for users? Will the outcomes last and be sustainable after the project has closed?
- **Practical feasibility**
  With the likely resources and time available, is it achievable?

Nine questions can help to shape a study.

1 Is it really needed?
2 Does it fit with other projects or activities?
3 Will it attract sufficient resources?
4 Is the financial basis of the project sound?
5 What assumptions can be made about likely income sources?
6 What about non-financial resources?
7 Is there a body of support for it?
8 Are the expected results realistic and worth the effort?
9 Does it fit with what we want to do?

Is it really needed?

All projects should be aimed at meeting a need and making some kind of sustainable difference. However, the history of voluntary and public sector projects includes several examples where a community's needs have been ignored, or a need was identified confusingly. Five things can go wrong.

1 Confusing needs and wants

Often, discussion about what people need is passive, general and influenced strongly by what the people commissioning the study want to hear. This happens when an established organisation decides to consult with its current or potential users, and the discussion is constrained by boundaries of the existing services and activities. What a person wants can be a different matter: it is more about personal choice, aspirations and preferences. It might be ambitious to focus on wants rather than needs, but often this leads to a much more creative and effective project.

CASE STUDY

A self-help agency consulted at length with the intended users of a new project. The results of the needs survey indicated that of the suggested services, daycare and counselling were the most needed. Six months later the project was set up. Attendance at the day centre and take-up of the counselling service were very poor, and a casual conversation with two potential users indicated a likely reason: the needs survey was general and impersonal. They had answered the questions by thinking about what they thought 'average' users would want. They personally would not want to attend a day centre or need counselling, but at the time it seemed sensible to suggest that others would.

2 Dealing with surface problems

A useful approach to needs analysis is to recognise that a problem may have different layers and only some are immediately obvious. For example, problems of juvenile street crime are likely to have a range of symptoms, problems and root causes. Lack of leisure facilities, youth unemployment, dysfunctional home life, inadequate policing, poor public safety and a lack of alternative role models are just some dimensions to the problem. It is easy to tackle only one or two dimensions (often the ones that you are most experienced or interested in) and ignore the deeper or more complex aspects. Researchers can be so interested in finding a solution that they do not spend sufficient time analysing the problem and challenging how it is presented.

3 Being fixed on the solution

Usually, a study is commissioned and carried out with a solution very clearly in mind: the problem is shaped to fit the solution. In one inner city area a respected community activist described what happens:

> We have had numerous vocational training programmes provided by central government. The courses have been good, but have not led to the economic regeneration that is needed. Indeed, some local people are now on their third or fourth course. Training is important, but it needs to go alongside job creation, small business support, childcare, transport on and off the estate and basic educational skills. However, all the recent research work has only looked at training and not at the whole picture.

4 Not really listening

Occasionally there is a tokenistic or cynical approach to research and consultation; it is done in order to produce credibility and evidence to win funding. The overt or inherent assumption is that the research will find nothing that would challenge the assumptions behind the intended project. The project is already designed: all that is needed is some evidence that it is wanted.

5 Coping rather than changing

A useful test in designing a project is to think about the overall vision behind it. What kind of sustainable impact will it make? Will the project really change things or will it merely make things more tolerable for a short period? Will the ideas behind the project make a real difference or will they only make a superficial change for a short period? What depth of intervention is needed? Is it better to do a few things that will create real change rather than spread resources widely and limit your impact to coping better?

Does it fit with other projects or activities?

A new project needs to be tested against existing or likely alternatives. Commercial organisations expect designers of new products to highlight their 'unique selling proposition' (USP). A USP is what your project can do or deliver that others do not. A similar process needs to be adapted to test out the fit between a possible new project and its environment. Two questions are worth asking.

1 Who else is doing similar or related work?

A useful technique is to map out all other agencies doing similar or related things to what you want to do. It is important when mapping other agencies, individuals, organisations and companies involved in the project's sphere to think broadly. Usually, one or two comparisons will be obvious, but others may be identified after some time.

2 Can the sector or market support a new project?

What is the size of the market for the project? Is it cluttered with other projects competing for funds and clients? Is there clear space for a new project? What are the main trends in the sector or market? Is it likely that demand for the project will increase, stand still or decline? Also, it is useful to compare the proposed project with existing or likely alternatives. What will be different about your project? What will it offer that will be distinctive?

Possible answers might point to what the project does and what it delivers, or how it works or its relationships to its users. You need to be clear how you will measure the difference, as the distinctive difference can be more about *how* you do something rather than *what* you do. Will its impact be greater or more distinctive? What will your project do that others do not? Will its impact be more relevant? Will it be more effective? Why will it work better?

If the project is unlikely to be much different or its impact similar to or the same as existing projects, then the question of its rationale must be raised. Why set up a new project if all it will do is what others are doing already?

Will it attract sufficient resources?

At the start of any new project this question is uppermost in people's thinking, and no certain answer is possible. Short-term funding programmes, changing priorities, political and economic uncertainty all make any long-term confidence about funding impossible. Conversely, this issue can be ignored by the promise or guarantee of initial funds for the first year or so (often with no guarantee of future funds). It is worth examining several aspects of this question.

Is the financial basis of the project sound?

Detailed costing at this stage is very difficult, but it should be possible to estimate the main costs involved in starting up and running the project. Are there particular aspects of the project where costs are likely to be unusually high or difficult to control?

What assumptions can be made about likely income sources?

The accuracy of the information you collect here needs to be evaluated: it is important to balance optimism and realism. Some projects do not get off the ground because they are unable to prove without a shadow of a doubt that they will attract funding. Others are backed at this stage on the basis of vague promises of funding from unnamed backers. It is worthwhile collecting three types of information.

1 Indications of definite or highly probable income

It may be that funders have indicated that they will back the project and provide funding or contracts. Unconditional promises can be hard to find and difficult to get on paper.

2 Feedback from potential funders

Informal sounding out from potential backers can be very helpful. The idea of the project, but not the detail of it, should be market tested. Possible funders or purchasers should be approached to comment on how the project would fit with their priorities. Do they recognise the need? Could they ever envisage backing it?

3 Evidence that the project can conform to relevant legislative or other standards in order to access statutory income

Increasingly, projects operate in a regulatory environment within which clear standards have to be met in order to operate and receive payment. Childcare, residential care and legal aid services are all examples of this. Meeting these standards will have cost, time and staffing implications. Unless the standards can be met, it is unlikely that the project will receive income.

Attention also needs to be given to the medium-term indications of funding. This may involve some realistic assessment of the stability of current income sources and the likely capacity to develop new income sources.

What about non-financial resources?

Is the project dependent on volunteers, resources given in kind or other hidden income? How safe are these inputs? What would happen to the project's costs if they were withdrawn or declined?

One project was set up to operate in a office donated by a local church and was dependent on a team of volunteers. Such support was taken for granted when the steering committee first discussed it. However, the appointment of a new vicar led to the project becoming homeless within its first few months, which in turn led to the volunteers drifting away and no new volunteers being recruited. In a few months the project went from being a promising one to a disaster. It had been set up 'on the cheap': there were no contingency plans or thought for what could go wrong, and it had assumed that goodwill would continue.

Is there a body of support for it?

A simple test is to map out the level of support for the project within different groups. Possible groups might include:

- direct users
- supporters
- decision-makers
- people indirectly affected by it.

There needs to be a critical mass of people who demonstrate a sense of ownership of, and commitment to, the project. They need to be prepared to invest their own time and effort in the project and be willing to fight for it. This can be a difficult issue to assess.

A steering group of people set up to develop an environmental project was well attended and seemed to have the basis of a strong core group. It had met together for nearly a year. The idea behind the group came from one person who had brought together all of the steering group; she did all the organising work, drafted the project's plan and marketed the project to others. Very little was delegated to other members of the group. When she was ill for three weeks, nothing happened – the planned steering group meeting went ahead, but it was embarrassing. No one knew what was happening, or even knew what needed to be discussed.

What this revealed was that the vision and concept of the project was held by only one person. It was felt that to set up a project on that basis was flawed and would create a very vulnerable project. For the project to move forward, the original innovator had to do less – others had to be involved, not just as a supporting cast, but as key players.

Are the expected results realistic and worth the effort?

A rough balance sheet needs to be drawn up to assess whether the work involved in setting up and running the project is likely to be paid back by the benefits generated. A traditional approach to this would be a value-for-money study. This involves testing the anticipated results against the following criteria.

- **Economy**
  Are the costs involved fair? Could it be done more cheaply?
- **Efficiency**
  If it were organised better, could we do more? Are the results worth the costs?
- **Effectiveness**
  Will it create real lasting benefit?

Such an approach depends on sufficient information being available. You also need to be able to make a fair comparison with other projects and have a clear sense of what value the project is trying to create.

An alternative and less financially driven approach is to predict realistically what difference the project will make in terms of what it creates and what it produces (the outputs), and what difference it will make for the users and society as a whole (the outcomes). Such predictions need to be discussed and explored carefully, and it is important to test if the project really will make a difference. Often projects are set up without a sense of what impact they will make.

A project to introduce the arts to isolated rural communities concentrated all of its efforts on reaching as many people as it could. It was felt that the issue of access was important and contact with high numbers would impress funders. The project's plan for the first two years would mean that people in each of the local communities would get only three to four two-hour sessions with the project. The actual value of this was questionable. Apart from a brief introduction to a new art form, what real skills or insights could be developed? The benefits of the project were not obvious or sustainable.

Does it fit with what we want to do?

It is possible that an idea for a new project is sound, viable and sustainable but not the right one for an existing organisation to set up. Three issues are relevant here.

1 Legal and constitutional fit

The activities involved in a new project could take the organisation outside of its remit. The 'aims and objectives' clause and the intended area of benefit may restrict the organisation from taking it on. For example, a charity's constitution may restrict it from operating outside a particular geographic area, or to working only with a particular client group. It may decide that it does not wish to alter its governing documents in order to broaden its remit.

2 Synergy

At some point, all the activities in an organisation need to connect up – they need to create a whole picture. If they do not, the organisation will become fragmented and lack purpose. New projects need to fit with other activities. As a director of a development agency commented:

> Three years ago we went through a dreadful phase. We stopped being a united organisation and became a loose collection of projects that had little relationship to each other. Some were very practical, some experimental, others were about policy and research. We lost our identity.

How broadly or how narrowly you seek synergy between projects may need to be discussed.

3 Skills and management fit

It may be that an existing organisation does not have the right balance of skills to manage the project, and may lack the structures to house it properly. If an existing organisation is unable to support or direct the project properly, then the chance of its success will be limited. If it is felt that the project is a good idea but in the wrong organisation, then options such as encouraging an independent project or transferring the idea to a more appropriate organisation should be considered.

Carrying out a feasibility study

Feasibility studies vary enormously in terms of scope, content and style. Some are the product of detailed independent research carried out to a strict methodology. Others are much more open-ended and deal more in people's opinions and impressions.

Types of studies

In broad terms there are three main types of study.

1 Needs-based

This type of study is focused much more on the need or problem identified than the proposed solution. It usually involves establishing exactly what problems exist, their size and extent and testing out how different solutions might overcome them. An example of this might be assessing the causes of family break-up in an area and from this research identifying the need for a family centre open at weekends.

2 Consultative

This type of study is about 'testing the water' for a project. When the study is commissioned it is usually clear what sort of project is intended or being actively considered. The aim of the study is to check that the project would be welcome, establish how best to organise and launch it, and to see how it can fit in best with other agencies. For example, a steering group of people concerned with legal rights might carry out a feasibility study to determine how best a law centre could operate in their city, what its priorities should be and how it should work alongside other advice agencies. The results of the plan will be used to shape their thinking as they develop their idea into a proposal.

3 Market-based

Often, this type of study is commissioned when the idea of the project is at an advanced stage. Its objective is to test out with potential funders, users or customers the details of how the project will operate, and it focuses on the detailed logistics and management of that operation. For example a new arts venue might commission such a study to assess anticipated audience levels, ticket prices and programme details. The findings of the study will play an important part in building up the centre's first business plan.

Designing a feasibility study

In designing a feasibility study, three main focuses can be used to develop specific questions.

1 Which of our assumptions about our idea need to be tested?

The most fundamental assumptions are rarely checked or explicitly stated. It is useful to list the information and data that you will need to consider the project further and work up a plan. Information needs could include:

- the current details of needs and local circumstances
- mapping other provision or similar activities
- available resources and their criteria.

2 What feedback do we need from other people about our idea?

Questions in this area relate more to people's reaction to the project. Possible issues here include:

- positive and negative reactions to the plan
- potential support, rivalry and opposition
- advice and ideas for the project.

3 Who should do it?

A feasibility study can be carried out by the people already involved in it, the people new to it or a combination. The people involved in the project already may be able to design and draw up a study and carry it out. It will be important that they are able to think about and describe the project objectively, rather than seeing the study as a way of selling the project.

Several external people and institutions undertake feasibility studies. Universities and colleges, consultancy practices and freelance consultants can offer some expertise. It is important to shop around and find out about particular strengths and past experience. In working with both internal and external people it is important that the terms of reference for the study are agreed and recorded clearly at this stage. They should list the areas that you would like to be studied, the specific questions that you need to have answered and the timetable for the exercise.

CASE STUDY

One organisation successfully used a combination of internal and external people to carry out a feasibility study on a planned new project. A small steering group of staff and committee members was set up to work alongside an experienced consultant. The consultant helped to clarify the areas to test and designed the methodology. Interviews and consultations were carried out by three placement students and volunteers, and the results were collated and analysed by the consultant. The steering group studied the findings and prepared a final report.

Gathering information

Good feasibility studies are able to deal with different types of information. A useful way of grouping different types of information is by way of 'hard' and 'soft' information. Hard information includes statistical data and factual information, such as census returns, relevant rules and regulations and quantitative survey returns, and soft information includes opinions and reactions. In developing a new project, good and relevant information is needed to check the accuracy of our understanding about needs and problems and show evidence of the need for the project.

Gathering information can be a long and exhausting task. There are particular dangers involved in overusing some sources of information, or not interpreting the findings fully. There is also a danger of overusing hard information and ignoring soft information sources.

Primary and secondary research

Primary research is information-gathering and studies of an issue or a need which have not been done before. You might choose to commission or carry out some primary research into an issue or need which it is believed has been unexplored or needs examining with a different insight. True primary research is unique and should have a line of enquiry which is unexplored. Primary research methods include:

- questionnaires
- postal surveys
- telephone surveys
- interviews
- group discussions
- case reviews.

Before commissioning original research, be sure that it really is original – there is no point in duplicating someone else's work. One way of finding out is to contact information officers in relevant organisations or to ask an experienced librarian to check research directories. If you decide to commission original research, make sure that you are certain you know what you want and why. All too often, research is commissioned because nobody knows what else to do with an idea or a project proposal. Be clear about your needs.

Research is not worth doing unless it is done well – and that can cost money, especially if it is original enquiry. In quantitative research, sample sizes often have to be high to get statistically valid results. Get advice from professional researchers before you start – it may cost, but you could save money in the long run.

Secondary research is carried out by collecting together, reviewing and interpreting relevant evidence, data and findings which have been researched and published by other parties. This information can be used to test out the project needs and ideas. There are many sources of published research. Careful thought needs to be given to their appropriateness to the project which you are developing.

Using the information

The following points need to be kept in mind when using statistical information. Surveys can gather information over such a wide area that they report on broad trends rather than specific needs. In addition, sometimes information arrives far too late for it to be useful. To make the research process and findings manageable, sometimes information has to be aggregated, and this makes intelligent interpretation hard. Research can raise as many questions as it answers.

Good information-gathering should use a mixture of hard information gathered by primary and secondary research and allow space and time for gathering non-quantitative factors such as feedback, opinions and preferences. Soft information is information that is not possible to reduce down to numbers. This could include people's emotional reaction to your idea, their personal preferences or opinions and odd bits of history, past experience or prejudice. The balance between the two is interesting. Nowadays, no computer manufacturer would launch a new system without taking into account factors such as 'user-friendliness' or the quality of design or appearance. Yet 10 years ago many computer manufacturers only concentrated on technical performance and capacity. The growth of the personal computer market was driven as much – if not more – by soft factors such as user-friendliness and accessibility. Getting the balance between hard and soft issues is critical now in determining the success of a product in the market. The project might be cost-effective, logical, well organised and well planned, but there needs to be a feeling of enthusiasm, goodwill and energy for it to work. Effective studies use a methodology which can pick up hard and soft information and ensure that it can be presented usefully.

Using the study's findings

The study's findings must be fed back quickly: there is little point in delaying since the basis of the findings is likely to change quickly. The document or report is only a part of the feasibility study. In addition, the people who worked on the study should be able to talk about their impressions and assessment of the information presented. The conclusions need to be talked through to see how they change the original idea or outline of the project. There needs to be a degree of discipline and objectivity in how this is done. Quite often, when presented with findings that challenge the original idea, over-enthusiastic and passionate innovators respond by questioning the methodology or validity of the study – they shoot the messenger.

A well-designed feasibility study can provide valuable background to the decision to proceed, but it cannot guarantee success or make the decision to go ahead for you.

Running a pilot project

A pilot project is a scaled-down version of the intended project, aimed at doing one or all of several things:

- field test the project to see if it works in practice
- run it to see what successful features can be passed onto other projects, and identify weaknesses that need to be solved before moving to a bigger scale
- interest potential backers and supporters by showing a scaled-down project in action – this is sometimes called a 'demonstration project'.

A project can be scaled down in several ways: it can operate in a narrower geographic area; it can work with fewer people; or it can limit itself in scope or remit.

Pilot projects need to be well designed. Thought needs to be given as to how long a pilot has to run in order to draw conclusions. It is difficult to design the pilot in such a way that it will be an accurate study in micro of the real thing. The following points should be built into the design of any pilot.

- **Make sure that the pilot can fail as well as succeed**
  Often, we learn more from things going wrong or not working out as intended. Pilot projects need to be encouraged to be experimental and seen as a learning process. The reality can be different. Often the pressure is on to get it right first time and be totally successful. Staff employed on a pilot can pick up a message that if it works, it will become permanent and will provide them with secure work. There is a belief that funders need to see a perfect working pilot before they commit themselves. These factors can hide learning, discourage experimentation and distort reality.

- **Make sure that the pilot is as real as possible**
  One national agency set up a pilot to demonstrate a strategy to involve young people in their communities. The 18-month pilot was a major success: it worked well, obtained a high profile, enthused people and prompted four neighbouring local authorities to agree to fund a project in their local area. The four local projects did not work out as anticipated. Take-up from young people was low. Huge amounts of time had to be spent fundraising and gaining access to key people rather than doing the work, and one project was closed early. One probable reason was that the pilot received such a high profile and interest which was impossible to replicate in the mainstream projects. The attention of external evaluators, visitors from other authorities and media interest all encouraged people to make it work. For the pilot, doors were opened, money found and resources provided; however, the four mainstream projects were unable to command this degree of attention.

- **Build in review points**
  It is important that learning and evaluation points are built into pilots. A variety of techniques such as diaries, review meetings, users' panels, external evaluations and interviews can be used to identify progress. They can help to find out what works and why and, most importantly, help any projects that may follow to learn from the pilot's experience.

Making the decision to go ahead with the project

Many projects just happen – no one ever really gave approval to them to go ahead. People just start them and only talk to others about them when they need to (usually to get money). This is not a totally disastrous state of affairs; it can produce creative and imaginative projects. However, it can produce chaos and disorganisation. At worst, projects that fail can threaten the credibility or viability of the rest of the organisation.

The decision-making process needs to be thought through carefully. The right people will need to be involved. People with organisational responsibility (trustees, directors and managers) and people with a significant stake in it (staff, users and possibly funders) may need to be involved. They will need to have the right level of background information and operate to the same criteria. The people involved in the early development of the project will need to be able to enthuse others to back it, and at the same time be realistic about potential problems or unknown elements. Several techniques exist to help this process, which is called project appraisal.

Risk analysis

All activity involves risk. The following five risks are common in many projects:

1 financial risk – costs could escalate or income fail to materialise

2 legal risk – if the project does not work properly, the organisation or individual trustees could face liabilities

3 credibility risk – if the project fails, the organisation's name and credibility could be damaged

4 user risk – if the project does not perform properly it could set back, harm or damage the users

5 delivery risk – the output of the project is not certain or within the project organisation's control: it depends on other people or factors.

The project can be evaluated under each of these risks. Likely risks are evaluated and action is taken to minimise the risk.

Attitudes to risk

We need to look at our attitude to risk. There are two extreme positions: an unrestrained and reckless attitude that ignores risks in the pursuit of the goal, and a punctilious and cautious attitude that will feel safe only with a project in which every possible risk has been reduced. Both approaches are ineffective.

One strategy is to use a 'waterline' technique. New projects can be developed as we think best, provided that they do not endanger the parent organisation sponsoring the new organisation. The 'waterline' is the integrity, core values, financial balances and profile of the organisation.

Worst case scenario

A worst case scenario is an exercise in which pictures are drawn of the worst things that could happen to the project, and what their effect and implications would be. Possible scenarios might include funding ceasing, key people leaving, a drastic increase in competition and other such crises. Worst case scenarios are a useful way of assessing risks and identifying the safety nets necessary to protect the project.

Will it work?

Using a focus group

Three examples of when testing an idea might have been useful:

■ 'Heavier-than-air flying machines are impossible.' (Lord Kelvin, President, Royal Society, 1895)

■ 'Everything that can be invented has been invented.' (Charles H. Duell, Commissioner, United States Office of Patents, 1899)

■ 'We don't like their sound, and guitar music is on the way out.' (Decca Recording Co., rejecting the Beatles, 1962)

Testing an idea need not be a major task involving huge surveys and questionnaires. One commonly used marketing technique is to run a focus group. Facilitators run a short discussion group with potential consumers and purchasers; the group needs to have only five or six members and meet once or twice. The facilitator outlines the idea to be tested, works through a list of structured questions and then encourages a discussion.

CASE STUDY

One estate improvement project used this technique by running six separate focus groups for children, young people, single people, parents, older people and other agencies working on the estate. Two independent consultants acted as group leader and recorder. Each session began with a brief presentation of different options for estate improvement. The project director was very pleased with the results:

We got much more useful information from the groups than we would have got from a survey. A lot of the most useful feedback was about people's preferences and informal opinions that a questionnaire cannot pick up. Many of the casual comments made about what would and would not work were the most useful ones. The groups were a conversation rather than a one-way exercise. We intend to use different focus groups throughout the project to monitor reaction.

Using a cost–benefit study

A cost–benefit study looks at all the potential costs and anticipated benefits from a project. It should look at all the costs and benefits – not just financial – and at short and longer-term factors. It is a useful tool for summarising complex information and helping people to reach a decision.

CASE STUDY

A national agency carried out a cost–benefit study of creating a publishing unit to produce a limited number of publications and books. The study summarised all the known costs and likely benefits.

Costs	Benefits
■ Start-up costs of £10,000	■ Our membership provides an instant base market for most publications
■ Break-even point will be year 2 or year 3 – would have to underwrite this venture for at least two years	■ We have a unique position in the market – no other publisher has our expertise or connections in this market
■ Price of each publication will have to be at least £10 to cover cost	■ Publications are an effective way of informing and profiling our work – this would support our agreed strategic direction
■ Publishing is a volatile business. Costs and market trends can change quickly	■ In three years' time we anticipate this venture being self-financing and possibly creating a small income source
■ Will need a part-time staff post in year 1	■ Publications will raise our profile. They will create broader interest, enhance public interest and media coverage

Analysis of the study can be built upon by adding a points weighting to each factor:

■ three points for very significant factors
■ two points for significant factors
■ one point for other factors.

This is useful in determining how people see the importance of each factor and in giving an overall sense of the total cost and benefit of a project.

Thinking and operating narrowly

A sports development project decided not to bid to a specification for a contract with its local health authority to develop a healthy lifestyles campaign. The project felt that the specification did not 'sound like us', although the actual work involved and the anticipated outputs and outcomes were almost identical to what it was doing currently. The specification was written in a health professional's language rather than a sports development one.

The board that would never say 'Yes'

At her leaving party, the coordinator of a regeneration agency described how trying to get her board to back a new project was hard, exhausting and deeply frustrating:

When presented with an idea for a project, their immediate response was to ask for detailed information. This was often followed by a request for a feasibility study or a written business case or a detailed risk analysis. I would go off and do whatever was requested. Once presented with this information, they would then suggest a pilot project to see if it would work. Constant requests for new information and more evidence was a good way of avoiding making a definite decision.

In the end I gave up progressing new ideas! By the time the board gave it the green light, someone else had already started doing it and any enthusiasm for it had been lost!

The board often asked for relevant information and were diligent in their responsibility for managing risk – but they need to recognise that they have a role to create an atmosphere that encourages new ideas and innovation rather than grinds people down.

Outline structure of a feasibility study

Introduction	Gives brief details as to how the study was commissioned: who carried it out and when?
Background	States why the study was carried out. Is the purpose to identify needs, check that a project would work or test the market for it?
Assumptions	Summarises the main assumptions for testing, supplied by those commissioning the study. Examples might include 'the belief that a particular need is not being met', that 'no other organisation is doing anything similar' or that 'this project could be self-financing'.
Issues tested	Lists the particular questions that need to be answered specifically and concisely, so that it can be assessed later whether the study has met the original needs. The study should include reference to the potential risks that the project might encounter, and assess whether the level of risk might outweigh the potential benefit.

Methodology	Notes when and how the study was carried out. It includes the different techniques used to gather information and the organisations and people that were contacted during the study.
Findings	Present the findings with as little commentary as possible. Thought should be given to how statistical information can be shown and how opinions and reactions can best be presented.
Observations	An outline of the main observations and any interpretation of the findings. This section should comment on any issues which may not have been part of the original brief, but which may have come to light during the study, as side issues can be very useful.
How the study can inform development of the plan	The findings are matched against any existing or proposed plan. In this section, attention is given to how the lessons from the study can be applied to any future project.
Conclusions and recommendations	Summarises the study and draws from it any specific recommendations for future action.

Just how innovative...

In 1993, Stephen Osborne of the Aston Business School carried out a research project into the meaning and extent of innovation within voluntary organisations operating in social welfare (Osborne, 1994), where 195 organisations from three areas took part in a survey. This was followed up by 24 in-depth case studies of individual organisations. The findings raise the question of the actual extent of innovation within the voluntary sector:

- 48% reported no innovative developments
- of those that did identify some innovation, 26% were of a developmental nature (the existing service is developed with the same client group) and 47% of the respondents described an evolutionary innovation (where new services are provided to an existing client group)
- 15% reported expansionary innovation (using an existing service with a new client group) and 11% identified total innovation (new services meeting the needs of a new client group)
- very few organisations claimed innovations of national significance.

The report suggested that these findings 'refute the commonplace view of voluntary organisations as all inherently innovative'. The follow-up case studies also found no inherent characteristic of a voluntary organisation which could predispose it towards innovative activity. Rather, the most significant factors were the expectations of key stakeholders within and outside the organisation (particularly their major funders) and how it chose to respond to these.

Eight reasons not to go ahead with a project

Organisations can be very reluctant to say 'no' to an opportunity. As one experienced voluntary sector trustee put it:

> It is not in my make-up to turn an opportunity down. I much prefer to jump in and have a go, although I am learning that this is often quite dangerous.

Here are eight reasons to say no to a project, presented via some examples based on real cases, with ideas about managing each one.

Reason	Example	Solution
1 The project is outside our aims	A charity was asked to take on a project working with a new client group that was outside of its constitutional aims.	Organisations need to ensure that all activities are in line with the aims and objects set out in their governing document. To go beyond these aims could be unlawful.
2 The risks are too high	A worker suggested a highly innovative and experimental project. If it worked it could be fantastic. However, failure could damage profile and credibility and be costly.	All risks need to be properly identified and their likelihood assessed. Work could be done on what steps could be taken to reduce the risk, or to have contingency plans in place, should a risk happen.
3 It does not fit with our agreed strategy	After a long internal process, the trustees of a voluntary organisation agreed to a three-year strategic plan which would focus the organisation on working with disadvantaged 13–19-year-olds. Three months after agreeing the plan, the organisation's fundraiser reported that he was confident that a major funder was keen to support a project with much younger children.	It is very easy for strategic plans to be allowed to drift or become only a 'paper document'. The process of developing the strategy should be one that involves people and helps them relate it to their work.
4 We do not have the skills or expertise to do it	An environmental project was encouraged to bid to run a project that would involve running community leisure facilities such as sport in a country park. The project did not bid because the proposal was felt to be outside its skill range.	All organisations have sets of skills and expertise that make up organisational competency. Solutions might be to develop partnerships or subcontract elements of the project to other agencies with the particular skill or expertise.
5 It is too short term	A health charity turned down a project to provide support to client group because the commissioner would commit only to a one-year contract with the possibility of renewal. The charity's management committee felt that it would be irresponsible of them to start a service that people might begin to depend on, just as the funding ran out.	With all fixed-term projects, organisations need to be satisfied that they can manage usefully the short-term nature of it, and that something sustainable and useful can be done in the agreed period.
6 The resources are inadequate	A local authority was reluctant to pay the full costs of a project. It would meet the direct costs but only a small element of the organisational costs involved in managing it.	To what extent is it realistic, safe or prudent to take on a project without all the costs being met? Is it reasonable for a charity to be expected to subsidise it or prop up the real costs?
7 The need is not understood fully	A statutory agency was keen to commission a project which it had based on what it assumed the client group wanted, without any detailed analysis or dialogue.	It can be dangerous to assume that the project sponsor really understands what the client wants or needs. Is there space and interest to develop the project brief and involve service users?
8 We are being 'bounced into it'	Keen to meet national targets and satisfy its political bosses, a local authority tried to put pressure on a voluntary organisation to take on a regeneration project. 'Their interest was more about being able to tick boxes and be seen to be doing something, rather than doing something that would make a difference.'	It is important to stand back and evaluate project plans rather than assume that they are relevant.

A risk analysis matrix

This matrix is a simple way of judging the risks involved in a project. It looks at the level of anticipated risks and compares it with the anticipated results. There are four steps in using the exercise:

1   decide on the project that you want to test

2   ask if it faces high risks or low risks

3   ask if the results are likely to be low, medium or high

4   use this information to allocate your project to one of the four boxes.

Risk matrix	Results	
Risk	Low/medium results	Medium/high results
High risks	Box 1 Are the results worth the risks?	Box 2 How can we protect ourselves against the risks?
Low risk	Box 3 Is it worth doing?	Box 4 Do it!

Possible risks are:

■   financial

■   legal

■   credibility

■   to the user.

Possible results are:

■   volume of services and activity

■   impact and outcomes

■   financial returns.

Box 1 projects (high risk and low/medium results) should be reviewed to see whether it is worth bothering with them. The level of risk outweighs the anticipated results.

Box 2 projects (high risk and medium/high results) may well be attractive, given some kind of safety net or contingency plan. Can the risk be reduced, shared, protected against or insured?

Box 3 projects (low risk and low/medium results) may lack any sense of challenge or innovation. Are they worth the effort?

Box 4 projects (low risk and medium/high results) look well worth backing, provided that the assessments of anticipated returns and results are accurate.

Project definition

The **project definition** stage should bring together all of the ideas and aspirations about the project and ensure that there is a clear understanding as to what the project is intended to achieve. The document should be written in a style which is sharp, active and realistic. A good project definition can be helpful in a number of ways.

- **It can manage and create expectations**
  A clearly worded and concise project definition can help people to see what the project is aiming to do, understand its scope and appreciate its limitations.

- **It can help to win support**
  Using the definition to talk to potential partners, backers and decision-makers can be a useful way of building up a body of support for the project.

- **It can involve people**
  The definition stage is more than producing a document; it is an opportunity to involve likely users, partners, colleagues and others. Often, the more that people are involved in the early stages, the greater the chance of them being supportive later.

- **It can create informed monitoring and evaluation**
  It is very difficult to measure a project without a clear and recorded definition of intended outcomes.

A project definition needs to convey the following aspects of the project.

- **The overall vision and values**
  The project definition needs to set out in simple terms the 'big picture' for the project. It needs to communicate what the project hopes to achieve, why it is important and the benefits that can be expected. In addition, it should highlight the core values or philosophy that underpins the project.

- **Evidence of needs**
  The need for the project should be set out by summarising the relevant facts and evidence. This should be kept brief but made as locally relevant as possible. It may be useful to link the needs to the local authority's targets or priorities (such as local area agreements) or indicate how the project will work alongside other organisations.

- **Evidence that the project's ideas have been tested and could work**
  Evidence of past work, your track record, experience of running similar projects and results of any feasibility studies should be summarised to indicate that the project is realistic and has been tested. It might be useful to indicate whether the project is part of a wider organisation and, if so, how the organisation adds expertise, support and value.

- **An outline of how the project will work and what resources it will need**
  A brief description should be made of how you envisage the project working, its location, staffing and outline financial plans. This need only be a basic sketch of how you anticipate funding the project: two or three well-designed pages should be sufficient to convey the main ideas. Its purpose is to stimulate interest and discussion.

Putting the definition stage together

The process of putting the definition together should be a participative and organised one. It should draw on the original idea behind the project and any feasibility or needs analysis work carried out. It is an opportunity to involve people and bring them into the project. However, it is important that the definition process does not drag on and that a tendency to say 'yes' to everything is avoided. Towards the end of the definition process, someone (either the project sponsor or a senior person in the host organisation) has to draw the process to a close and agree the project definition.

A good project definition is made up of the following:

- agreement about the project's intended outcomes
- agreement as to what success is
- agreement as to the scope and remit of the project.

About outcomes

Over time there has been considerable interest and some confusion about the idea of basing programmes and projects on outcomes. Outcome planning and measurement shifts the focus from the activity and output (what you do and deliver) to what the project changes and the difference that it makes.

A simple model

A well-established way of evaluating and measuring the work of an organisation is to describe it as a flow chart:

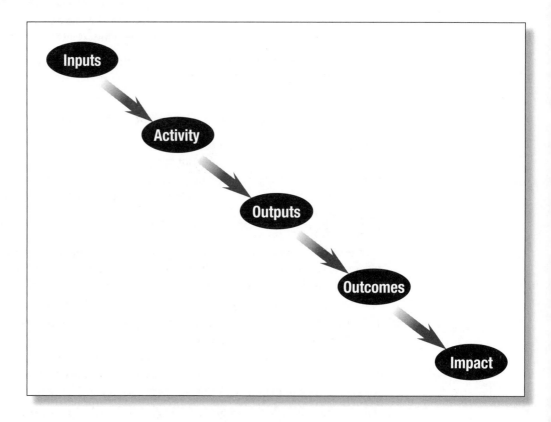

Defining the stages

Stage	Definition	Example
Inputs	The resources allocated and used to deliver the project.	Examples might include funding, time and any other resource used to set up and deliver the project.
Activity	What the project does.	Activities might include giving advice, organising an event or running a training session.
Outputs	What the project delivers.	The outputs are usually easy to quantify – examples could include the number of sessions delivered, the amount of support given and the number of training sessions run.
Outcomes	The difference, changes and benefits gained by the user as a result of the project.	The outcomes are the changes that the outputs cause – it is possible to identify different kinds of outcomes. Some are about change, helping a user to get something they want, changing behaviour or developing a new skill. Some outcomes are *preventative* – stopping something from happening, such as preventing environmental decline or stopping a situation getting worse. Others might be *learning* outcomes, such as finding out if a new approach works.
Impact	The impact is the longer-term effects of the project.	Examples could include policy and practice changes in service providers as a long-term consequence of the project, or contributing to achieving bigger policy targets such as building a stronger local economy or improving local health.

Outcomes can happen at different levels. It is possible to identify outcomes for individual users, groups, services and other stakeholders in a project. A successful project might lead to positive changes in an individual user's circumstances. Also, statutory agencies might meet their policy objectives by supporting a project. Some outcomes create tangible differences, for example, getting a job or improving the physical conditions of a local area. Others can be more about feelings and perceptions, such as increased confidence or self-esteem, or a stronger sense of community pride.

In the past, many organisations and funders have focused entirely on the inputs and outputs. Measurement systems have been inclined to count the quantity of the outputs and avoid more demanding questions, such as: did it make any difference? What has changed as a result of what we did? Funding agreements and service contracts have been structured around the output, for example: 'to create x number of training places' or 'to be open for y number of hours per day'. The shift to outcomes has a number of implications.

- **Is the intended outcome clear?**
  Often we focus so much effort on managing the output that we overlook the outcomes. It is useful to start planning work and funding bids by highlighting the expected outcomes.

- **Is there a shared agreement about the outcomes?**
  Sometimes conflicts and tensions can occur if people have different views or expectations as to what the outcomes should be. Ideally users, funders and the host agency should have a similar view of the intended outcomes, or at least recognition of overlapping outcomes.

- **Measuring outcomes is harder that counting outputs**
  Outputs are much easier to count, quantify and record. They are usually straightforward and unambiguous. Outcomes can be harder to quantify: measurement of an outcome requires a judgement, for example: 'Do I now feel more confident . . . ?' rather than a simple tick-box approach.

- **Lasting outcomes take time**
  Outcomes need to create some lasting change. For an outcome to make a significant difference, it might take time. Outcomes should not be quick fixes, they should last.

- **Some outcomes might not have been planned**
  As mentioned previously, often some of the most significant outcomes are the product of side-effects or things that were not in a plan. A user going on to set up a user group or undertake an educational course might not have been planned or anticipated at the start, but both outcomes are very worthwhile. Outcome monitoring needs to take a wider view and be able to spot and record side-effects and unplanned outcomes.

Focusing on outcomes at the start of the definition stage is a good way to clarify the result of the project. Examples of outcomes include:

- a newly-established residents' and tenants' association capable of managing its own affairs

- more young people participating in organised sport

- long-term unemployed people in a better position to get jobs.

The move to outcomes requires a change in how we think, plan and manage projects. Here are some of the key changes.

Greater clarity

Are we clear which outcomes we are working towards? How can we be sure that what we do leads to an outcome?

Capacity to work to the same outcome

The outcomes might depend on the contribution of several people and different agencies. Can we ensure that there is a shared understanding of the intended outcomes?

Who says what a 'good outcome' is?

A key issue is who says which outcomes are important. An advocacy service can deliver many hard and soft, short and long-term outcomes for different people. How do we ensure that the user has a principal role in determining which outcomes are relevant and should be monitored?

Success criteria

A very practical technique in developing a project is to draw up project success criteria. Success criteria set out how success will be judged at the end of the project. They should describe the main factors that people will use to determine whether the project has delivered. Often, success criteria are a mixture of two types of success:

- hard factors – these are the easier ones to audit, as they relate to the project's outputs and what it has delivered. Hard criteria include the following: did the project meet its deadlines? Did it keep to budget? Did its output meet with expectations and conform with the original specifications and legal or technical requirements?

■ soft factors – these require more judgement and feedback from users and others. Often they relate to process matters, such as: did the project keep people informed? Did the project support people through change?

Getting the balance right between the hard and soft factors can be an interesting exercise. For example, the director of a medium-sized charity sponsored a project to bring in a new communications and information system to help different offices work better and share information more effectively. He commented:

At one level the project did what we asked it to: it designed and implemented a system that was delivered on time and on budget. However, the way that it did it left a lot to be desired. Staff felt, and still feel, uninvolved in the process. People don't feel competent in using the system. The failure to manage the process has damaged the success of the whole project.

Often, the soft factors are critical in ensuring that the work of the project is sustained once the project has closed.

Success criteria can be a very positive tool to use in the definition stage. In not-for-profit agencies, words such as 'success' are not used enough. This tool gives people working on the project something to aim at, and it aids planning. The technique centres on the relatively simple but challenging question: 'At the end of it, how will we know that the project has been a success?'

Asking this question of different stakeholders can help to clarify people's hopes and aspirations for the project. People often find it easier to talk about what they do not want – this is useful, but a project needs to be built on a positive vision rather than an entirely negative one.

CASE STUDY

An example of project success criteria

A small project set up to improve and develop the skills of voluntary management committees drew up the following success criteria for its two-year project.

Hard criteria

■ 300 trustees will be trained in their role and legal responsibilities
■ a core training programme, resource bank and other material capable of being passed on to other network agencies will be in place at the project's end
■ up to four trustee support networks will have been established and will be able to carry on meeting without external support
■ at least six local bodies' good practice consultancies will have been carried out and the main learning points of these studies will have been disseminated
■ the funds and resources will be secured to ensure that trustee training will continue to be available in some form locally
■ a network of individuals and organisations able to demonstrate good practice and provide training and support to other groups will be in place.

Soft criteria

■ a measurable improvement in the quality of governance and management within the local voluntary sector
■ fewer conflicts within agencies as a result of disagreements over roles and relationships
■ increased awareness of the importance of good management practice and good governance in local agencies
■ the management of this project will be an example of good practice from which others can learn.

Managing the definition stage

Managing the definition stage requires particular skills and discipline. Sometimes projects suffer or even fail because the definition stage has been rushed or done in a very superficial way. Project managers either rush or are pushed into the delivery stage, then have to spend time redefining what was actually wanted. Here are six practical ways to manage the definition stage.

1 Avoid purely number targets

There is more to life than number-crunching. Defining a project only in numerical terms rarely covers the whole picture. For example, the original definition for an organisation's fundraising project was to 'raise £70,000 this year'. After discussion, this was amended to 'deliver a project that opens up at least three significant (c. £20,000 per year) new income streams that will be sustained in the medium term'.

Simple number targets can encourage people to 'watch the scoreboard and not the game'.

2 Manage expectations

Part of the definition process is negotiating with the different stakeholders and managing their expectations of the project. After consulting and listening to people it is important to go back to them, show that you have listened, and then demonstrate their views have shaped the project. In some cases this might mean having to explain to people that the project is not going to be able to deliver exactly what they wanted. As one community activist commented:

We are forever being asked to input into the design of a new project, but no one ever comes back to tell us how our views influenced, or did not influence, the plan.

3 Watch out for hidden agendas

Hidden agendas cover all the unsaid concerns, fears and aims. For example, one experienced project manager reflected:

Probably all the projects I have been involved in have had hidden agendas that are not stated at the project definition stage. Some are about history: 'We see organisation x as a rival and want to beat them'; others are about ego or game-playing: 'I want to get lots of good coverage in the local media.' Often people genuinely overlook things, feel reluctant to talk openly about what really matters, or assume that somehow or other I can read their mind! If the issues on the hidden agenda are not brought out into the open, the project is likely to suffer.

Asking probing questions, testing things out and looking at what is driving the project can help to identify hidden issues.

4 Keep it simple

Tear up definition documents that refer to 'the project creating user-focused, best practice, integrated and dynamic interventions'. Keep the success criteria brief. Writing them in headlines on one side of paper is much more useful than having lots of detailed criteria. The language needs to be active and unambiguous – avoid jargon and explain clearly what the project is going to do.

5 Record it

It is vital that the project definition is fully recorded and circulated to all those who have contributed to it. A concise record of the project definition stage will enable the project to plan implementation, monitor progress and evaluate results.

6 Seek active agreement

Just because someone came to a project meeting does not mean that they are committed to it. It is useful to check that key players such as the sponsor and host organisation fully understand the definition stage and actively are supporting it. One tactic is to ask key players to sign up to the project definition document.

Mapping a project's stakeholders

Stakeholders are the people and organisations with an interest in the project. The interest might be positive or negative, or it might be realistic or unrealistic. Identifying and analysing stakeholders can be a useful way to spot potential problems and work out how the project might need to communicate, manage change and deal with potential blocks and barriers.

For example, 'Offbeat' was a project set up by a charity to do work in schools on alternatives to violence. It worked with Year 10 and 11 students by offering a programme of four hour-long sessions spread over six weeks. The project was funded by a charitable trust interested in encouraging peaceful solutions. It is hoped that the project will become self-funding by being able to charge schools and local authorities (LAs) for the programme.

At the beginning of the project, 12 stakeholders were identified:

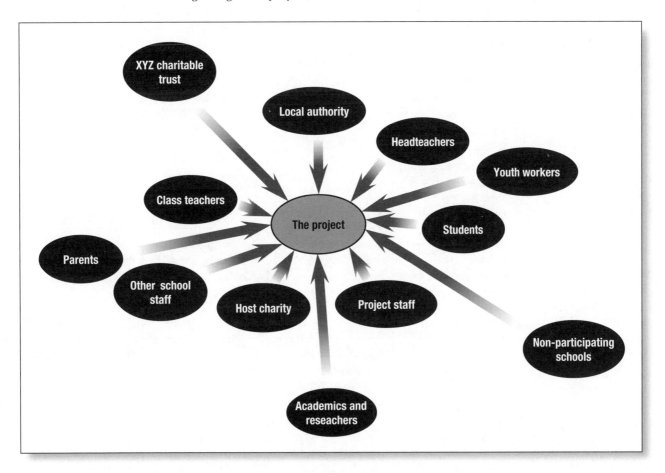

The analysis looked like this:

Stakeholder	Interest in the project	Concerns or negative interest	Future interest or role	Action points
XYZ charitable trust	It is committed to fund the project for the next three years. Interested in this work.	Lots of other projects competing for the trust's attention. Danger that it will move on after this funding.	Might it be interested in helping to roll out or scale up this successful project? Make its initial investment go further.	Need to involve the trust in the project evaluation process and early discussions about exit strategies.
Local authority	Has indicated support for this project. Currently makes no direct contribution to it.	Could this be seen as yet another initiative?	It needs evidence that this project works. LA advisers could be key in persuading other schools to invite us in and identifying ways of funding the project.	Need to develop good evidence. Make contact with LA advisory staff. Talk to them about funding models and how the project might be funded.
Headteachers	Central role. Often make or recommend the decision to invite us in. They must be committed to it. Need to show how the project can tackle real school problems, e.g. bullying and behaviour. Heads want recognition from agencies such as Ofsted that this is a good initiative.	Concern that they might want a 'quick fix'. Have they the time to work with the project?	They will have a key role in taking the project forward. Heads could have a valuable role in encouraging other heads to take on this project.	Need to ensure that they are involved and kept in touch with progress. Encourage write-ups of success stories in local and national media. Talk to friendly and supportive heads about how best to access their networks.
Youth workers	Several have expressed an interest in the project – including the possibility of running the scheme in non-school settings.	Is there a danger of taking on too much?	Consider possible ways of developing and extending the project in 18 months' time.	Find ways of keeping them in touch with the project.
Students	The beneficiaries. The project should give them skills and strategies to change their behaviour and challenge others.	Although in the main they enjoy the programme, does it really make a long-term and sustained difference?	Need to do or commission some follow-up research.	Find ways of measuring outcomes.
Non-participating schools	May have heard of the project. Increasingly recognise that violence is an issue.	Interested, but worried about: ■ time involved ■ cost ■ whether it will work.	Hopefully they can be encouraged to invite us in.	We should develop a marketing campaign that shows: ■ results ■ costs and work involved ■ how it could be funded.

Stakeholder	Interest in the project	Concerns or negative interest	Future interest or role	Action points
Project staff	Employed to work on the project until the funding dries up.	Worried about insecurity.	Need to work on exit plan.	Keep them informed about progress.
Academics and researchers	Several interests in the project. Always on the look-out for new and emerging practice.	We must remain a practical project.	They could help us get profile and recognition.	Invite some onto our steering group. Regularly feed them progress updates.
Host charity	The host agreed to take on the role of managing and supporting the project. It handles the money, employs the staff and takes the risk.	Danger of the project becoming distant and out of touch with the host.	If the project grows, should it become independent?	Need to review the relationship on a quarterly basis.
Other school staff	Other school staff – e.g. caretakers and cleaners – need to be involved.	Tendency for them to be overlooked – this can cause resentment.	Find ways of developing a whole-school approach.	Run a briefing session for non-teaching staff about the project.
Parents	They need to see that the project is relevant and important.	They may not see the project as relevant.	Parents can be helpful in supporting change.	Produce materials for parents.
Class teachers	They should help the project to deliver and work with their class. They can provide valuable insight and practical support.	Danger that they see the project as being a way of getting time off, or that it is irrelevant.	Teachers should be able to identify behavioural change.	Consider developing a teacher–project agreement, and show how the project can link into curriculum targets.

What's the link?

A manager of a neighbourhood centre described how her organisation connected its projects:

On paper, the range and variety of our projects is huge. We have projects up and running to do with arts, community safety, sport, green spaces improvement and job training. Sometimes people find it hard to see what they all have in common.

A crucial part of my role is about ensuring that all of our projects are part of a bigger picture. I continually work with project workers to ensure that all projects are about two things. First, improving people's opportunities and life choices, and secondly, that all of the projects must find real ways of involving local people as participants and not just as recipients of services.

It's reassuring that when I do bring project workers together through training days or by encouraging skill sharing it is always notable what projects have in common and what they can learn from each other.

Who says what the outcome is?

The Castlerigg Centre won backing from a government agency to manage a three-year project to support local people in setting up their own business as a way out of unemployment. Six months into the project, the monitoring officer at the agency visited the project and suggested that it should begin to measure outcomes rather than simply record how many people it saw and how much advice and training it gave. The monitoring officer suggested that 'the number of clients seen by the project who then go on to set up a new business' would be an obvious outcome.

The project worker challenged this. On reflection, some of the clients she saw had practically no chance of creating a successful business. Many clients had disorganised or chaotic lives, and their business ideas were at best highly optimistic. They often lacked the skills or experience to be self-employed. To encourage them to set up a business (just to meet a target) could be disastrous and could put them into greater debt. In fact, in some cases, persuading a client not to become self-employed and to do something else such as go to college would be a much more successful outcome.

Why do they want it?

Here are some simple questions:

Why	Background?
	What is driving it?
	Needs and wants?
Who	Who has a direct or indirect stake in it?
	Who needs to be involved?
	Who could block progress?
What	What is the scope or boundary of the project?
	Shared outcomes?
	What must it deliver?

'Everything and the kitchen sink' planning

The Gollan Centre management committee was committed to community participation and active involvement. It wanted to ensure that communities were actively involved in designing and planning all new programmes and projects. With this in mind, Sue, a development worker, organised a consultation event of interested parties to help her develop ideas for a children's project for which the Centre had recently secured funding.

Sue was pleased with the turnout at the first meeting: 16 people from statutory agencies, local groups and groups with which the project could work attended. After a short introduction from Sue, the meeting began to make suggestions as to the scope, purpose and potential work of the project. Sue made a point of being very encouraging and welcomed any and all ideas. Most of the ideas were positive and helpful, but Sue began to feel that some people were pursuing their personal interests or hobby horses. As the meeting went on, Sue became increasingly concerned. Ideas were coming thick and fast, but many – such as running parenting classes or a summer festival – were way beyond the project's original role or remit. At the end of the meeting, Sue thanked people for participating and agreed to reconvene in three weeks' time.

In the few days after the meeting, Sue had a number of conversations that worried her. There was clearly a level of interest in the project; some of the people that Sue talked to clearly believed that because the consultation meeting discussed their ideas and had been so positive, they were going forward into the project plan. The way that people described the project now had little relationship to what Sue had agreed with the sponsor. Sue felt as if the project was being hijacked.

In the run-up to the next consultation meeting, Sue had to spend time talking to people about the constraints and limits of what the project could do. This involved some fairly difficult discussions, as some people felt that the consultation process was much more open. Sue reflected that, in future, she needed to be much clearer about what is and is not up for consultation, in order to ensure that false or unrealistic expectations were not created for the project.

Project papers

Sample project definition

Use this document to clarify the project definition stage. It focuses on:

- the idea behind the project
- the need for the project and the background to it
- draft anticipated outcomes.

Give a brief description of the overall idea behind this project
A project to find new ways to encourage young people to volunteer on the East Side estate.

What evidence is there that this project is needed?	What are the main factors driving this idea?
Research reports show that young people are not attracted to traditional volunteering roles and structures. Reports from organisations on East Side indicate a shortage of volunteers in the 16–25 age range.	Strong commitment to encouraging volunteering in the local area agreement.

What outcomes are anticipated as a result of this project?
- More young people volunteering - Stronger voluntary and community organisations on East Side - Stronger sense of community involvement and pride - Gains for volunteers – new skills, new opportunities - Better practice and understanding of how to engage young people in their communities.

What involvement have intended users had in developing the project idea?	What further work needs to be done to develop this idea?
Planning meeting on East Side attended by 10 young people.	Find out what has been tried in other areas. Identify possible funding streams. Further consultation.

Next steps involved in developing this project idea
Research funding and develop project proposal.

Project papers

Sample project approval

Use this document to seek organisational agreement to go ahead with the project. It focuses on:

- how the project fits with the organisation's strategy
- the risks, resource implications and organisational issues involved in taking on the project
- the potential benefits involved in the project.

A three-year project to encourage young people to volunteer

What are the success criteria for this project?

More young people volunteering on the East Side estate

Good quality volunteering placements for young people

Improved capacity to reach out to young people

How does this project fit with our strategic plan?

One of the six strategic priorities set out in the business plan is to actively promote volunteering

Describe what the project would do (timescale, staffing, key activities)

A three-year project employing one worker

The project would assess the current state of volunteering, consult with young people, design and deliver a recruitment campaign and find ways of supporting young volunteers

The project would work with agencies to help them develop strategies to work with young people

Resource implications (likely costs, infrastructure costs, etc.)

Staff cost: £26,000

Project costs: £20,000

Management costs: £7,000

Costed on a full-cost recovery basis

How will the project be resourced?

Agreed at this stage	Anticipated
Some interest from a local charitable trust	Application to the Big Lottery Fund

What are the likely resource costs to the organisation of this project?	Indicate and assess the key risks involved in this project
Office space Supervision costs	Failure to support volunteers in the long term – medium risk

What will happen after the project?	Involvement of any other partners?
Organisations should be in a stronger position to work with young volunteers	Discussions ongoing with neighbouring volunteer bureaux Strong interest from the Council's Youth Service

Type of approval requested	Decision
Agreement to start making funding applications	

Building the case

This chapter looks at the work involved in building support and backing for the project. The purpose of this stage is to create and win active support for the project in the hope that the support will lead to funding and resources being allocated to the project. The work at this stage involves building relationships with different people and agencies and being able to bring in a wider support base for the project than the people who had the original idea.

The time involved in this phase can vary from a matter of weeks to a year or more. It needs to be carefully monitored, with progress evaluated and tasks reviewed. This stage is more than just getting funding; experience suggests that organisations need to build alliances, develop support and then make funding bids.

Creating a steering group

A common first step in developing support is to set up a steering group. A small group of committed people is probably of more use than a larger group with differing levels of interest in, and commitment to, the idea behind the project. The group needs to have the time to devote to setting up, running and building support for the project. Membership might include potential users, experts in the field and practitioners. It may well be that this group will go on to become the project's first management committee, trustees or board.

A good steering group needs the right balance of relevant knowledge, contacts and expertise in funding and organisational management. All members need to have commitment to the project's vision and values. It may be possible to have people seconded to the group to develop the project, or to use a consultant to aid the process.

The group needs to be task-orientated, concerned about progress and able to build enthusiasm for the project – it should not be seen as yet another committee or meeting to attend. Setting a time-limit to the steering group stage often works well. If the group cannot get the project moving in, for example, nine months, then the whole idea may need to be reconsidered.

The job of the steering group is to win support for the project and create momentum for its establishment. The group should be convened and managed by the host organisation. Three issues around project steering groups need to be managed.

1 It needs to stick to the agreed project definition

It is not helpful if the group continues to add ideas or expands the brief. Its role is to help get the project up and running, not to increase its definition.

2 Members of the group need to recognise and acknowledge potential conflicts of interest

For example, someone might find themselves playing different roles as a member of the steering group working up a project funding proposal and as an employee of another agency that could be bidding for the same work.

3 The role and powers of the steering group should be delegated clearly

It is useful if the group advises the host organisation on how the project will operate, manage and perform. As mentioned in previous chapters, the host organisation has legal and constitutional responsibility for the project's affairs, and such responsibility cannot be delegated or transferred to the steering group.

Building a network of support

A common tactical error is to see developing support and external contacts solely in terms of getting cash. Funding tends to follow only after a relationship has been built and a common interest established. The objectives for this stage are to identify and make contact with people who may back the project now or in the future.

A useful technique is to map the different people or organisations that are important to the project or have influence on its success. This techniques is called 'stakeholder mapping': it can help to identify partners, manage communication and expectations and look at how a positive relationship can be formed with different players. Potential stakeholders might include:

- intended users and people connected to them
- sources of income
- supporters or volunteers
- decision-makers
- regulators
- relevant communities
- potential partners and allies.

It is possible to map out your current relationship to them and their investment or interest in the project. From this it is useful to develop a strategy to market the project and develop a useful relationship.

For example, a community development project has used this technique on several occasions. Its development manager described how the project works:

As we develop a project in a new area, we make up a list of all the people who are, or should be, significant to us. We spend time visiting them, explaining the project and asking for comments. We look at how we can overcome potential problems or correct misconceptions. I think that it is important to be open with people about our plans and be prepared to listen. Time spent building relationships early on always pays off.

It is worthwhile to look out for potential conflicts and tensions in the map. For example, a new project to open a hostel in a residential area may be able to predict some prejudice or anxiety from local neighbours. It needs to develop a strategy to manage this and create an effective relationship, or at the very least to minimise damage.

Analysing project stakeholders can lead to the following action:

- identifying what relationships need to be improved or repaired
- working out how best to manage communications and who the project needs to have on board
- highlighting potential conflict
- identifying which stakeholders the project can use to open doors for it and influence decision-makers.

Building a financing strategy

Questions about who will pay for or fund the project can crop up far too early. They block creativity and innovation, and are dealt with before the project's idea has been thought through properly. The cloth is cut to fit the price. It is important that the project definition is worked out before issues of financing are addressed.

The next chapter will go on to to look at the detail of costing a project. At this stage, it is important to explore the different types of income available, draw up an outline cost structure and develop a strategy to ensure income.

CASE STUDY

Thinking strategically about funding

Hashmere Skills Centre appointed a new director. The centre was well established and managed four projects, all of which were connected in some way to economic and community development. In his first few weeks the director realised that the way in which the centre raised money for projects was at best confused, and at worst, chaotic. Three particular problems were evident:

- projects were undercosted
- enormous effort went into chasing tiny amounts of money
- the centre did not manage its relations with the people who funded its work.

He persuaded the management board to set up a team to review and develop a strategy for funding future projects. Three members of the board worked with him. They reviewed previous projects, looked at how projects had been costed and interviewed representatives from their main funding bodies. Their report and recommendations were sharp.

One of the centre's main income sources was the Learning and Skills Council (LSC). The LSC staff knew very little about what the centre did: they rarely visited it and only received formal monitoring information about the statistical performance of projects.

The relationship with several of the centre's backers was confused and out of date. The centre used terms such as 'fundraising' and 'grant-aid contribution' and referred to the backers as 'funders'. The various bodies which supported the centre's projects wanted a much more active relationship than simply 'putting up the money'. They wanted a partnership that was centred on developing joint initiatives, sharing ideas and know-how and learning from each other. One programme manager commented that the only correspondence he ever had from the centre was requests for money.

The centre's backers needed to know (and good management suggested that the centre ought to know as well) exactly what a project would cost. They were not interested in making a financial contribution to the centre's overall running costs, in the hope that it would trickle down into projects. They had to know that their budget was being used to sponsor projects relevant to their objectives, accepting that a 'reasonable amount' could be paid as a management fee to the centre.

The management board recognised that this approach would require a different approach from the centre: they would have to spend more time on getting and keeping project backers. Over six months the centre took four main initiatives:

1 it implemented a marketing plan, whereby key individuals from current and potential backers were invited to the centre and encouraged to see themselves as investors in its success

2 potential backers were consulted at the ideas stage of a project rather than simply being asked to fund it – their advice was sought and reactions welcomed

3 a newsletter for 'partners' was developed – this bulletin gave quarterly information on developments at the centre, progress reports and success stories. It was circulated widely in partner agencies, rather than to their named contact officers, and its objective was to raise the profile of the project

4 the centre has moved away from a traditional budget and adopted a cost-centre framework, where each project is a centre – all costs are allocated to, or shared out among, the cost centres. For the first time, the full cost of running a project – and of some fundraising – was known.

The centre director can point to the early results of this plan:

We do have a much closer relationship with our sponsors. In some cases we have had to do all of the work and force our way in. We are now being invited to work with them in a much more collaborative way, which is leading to some new (and properly resourced) projects.

Balancing different types of income

Getting money for a project takes up an increasing amount of time. Policies, criteria and practices change regularly. In many instances, the term 'funding' is becoming out of date and being replaced by contracts and agreements. The relationship is changing from that of grant giver and grant receiver to one based on carrying out a defined piece of work in return for a fee. Often an investment or a partnership relationship is preferred to the historic one of benevolent funder and worthy supplicant.

Balancing income is also harder. Many sources of income are becoming targeted increasingly and are reluctant to fund what traditionally has been called 'core costs' such as administration and management. Some income may be restricted or earmarked so that it can only be spent in an agreed way. There are four main sources of income.

1 Statutory sources

Traditionally, central and local government have grant-aided projects to provide support. This relationship is in a state of flux. Several local authorities and health authorities have moved into a contractual relationship with voluntary organisations. Central government increasingly regards voluntary projects as being part of the network that delivers its programme rather than a 'good cause to fund'. Often, central government creates programmes and initiatives which are rolled out through different partners, and these initiatives lead to projects delivered by local or specialist partners. Open-ended grants, where the public authority agrees to fund a project without stipulating what strings will be attached, are few and far between for new projects.

2 Trusts and foundations

The vast range of charitable trust, corporate funding and other foundations operate in very different ways: some are quite secretive in their affairs and operate mainly through personal contact and recommendation; others have clear criteria and processes for awarding grants. In this category (although practically a category on its own) sits the National Lottery. The lottery distribution boards have transformed and increased the opportunities available to fund new projects.

3 Public fundraising

The different methods of raising money from known supporters and the public at large are well documented and continually expanding. Public fundraising in its various guises has become much more competitive, and consequently expensive. Shifting trends in giving and changing public opinion make reliance on regular public fundraising an unlikely option for many projects.

4 Earned income

Provided that voluntary organisations keep within their charitable objectives, the capacity to earn income through selling services exists. This can take the form of charging for activities through rent income, fees, charges and trading. Projects which plan to rely heavily on earned income should test the market first, understand how it works and be able to make informed judgements about how they will operate within the market.

In developing a finance strategy, various issues need to be considered.

Statutory versus voluntary

A difficult policy issue is how to define what activities should be regarded as statutory functions – that is, which the central or local state should provide directly or under contract – and what activities should be met through voluntary or charitable purposes. To what extent, if at all, should a project use resources provided by supporters and charitable income to support, complement or enhance services that might be expected to be statutory? For many agencies this has been a tricky line to draw.

Dependency

Is there a danger of a project being overreliant on one main funding stream? How stable is the funding stream? What would happen if policies and priorities changed? Can the project find a way of developing a broader spread of income?

Short-term and long-term income

Few sources of income offer projects the safe prospect of long-term, guaranteed funding upon which to build long-term sustainable activities. Short-term funding can be hazardous. Several projects have been delighted by the interest and backing that they attract when they are new, only to find that the interest is not there even as soon as two years down the road. Often, being 'new' is a convincing reason why projects attract income. A project needs to weigh up the risks involved in starting up without strong indications of long-term funding, or it must design its organisation so that it can be scaled down or closed without harm.

Earmarked and non-restricted funds

Projects can be started as a result of money becoming available which can only be spent on a particular activity. Examples might include statutory sources that restrict expenditure by criteria of geography, client group or activity, or income from fundraising where the donor has granted it on the express understanding that it can be spent only on a particular activity. The relationship between restricted and non-restricted funds is a tricky one. Overreliance on restricted funds can mean that the project becomes distorted – it is rich only in some parts.

The coordinator of a health project described how restricted funds caused problems for his new project:

> Over 45% of our income for the first two years came from an NHS contract for work with young people. This money was tightly monitored by the local primary care trust [PCT], who insisted that it could only be spent on work with young people. This caused two problems for us. First, the issues we worked on were not particular to young people, but we had to bend the way we described and monitored our work to fit the contract's restriction. Secondly, the PCT were reluctant to allow for more than seven per cent of the fee to go on project management costs. This caused us major problems when costing for other activities. Other projects had to contribute much more towards admin costs. In effect, they subsidised the management costs of our work with young people.

An outline cost structure

At this stage you need to work out in broad terms how much the project will cost: this need not be a detailed exercise, but you will need outline figures to discuss with potential backers. Costing techniques are discussed later in this book, but it is important not to underestimate the outline cost of the project. Promises made here that the project will operate on a low cost may come back to haunt you later.

Funding strategy

Fundraising is now an industry. Consultancies and professional fundraisers are keen to offer advice, information and expertise for a fee. However, it is important that devising a funding strategy for the project is a mainstream consideration rather than something which is delegated to a fundraiser. The funding strategy needs to be informed by the following:

- the project definition
- the host organisation's business plan
- the anticipated balance of income sources for the project
- the outline cost structure of the project.

Many organisations waste time in fundraising by failing to have any clear sense of strategy and becoming driven by being busy rather than being effective. The following form the basis of an effective strategy.

Research and test first

Do not judge your fundraising work by the volume of activity that you undertake: much fundraising effort is worthy, but wasted; the level of work involved does not merit the return. It is important to spend time researching the possible income sources available, finding out about relevant criteria and practice and deciding how best to make an approach. One national project employed a consultant to develop its funding strategy by testing the project on six possible local authority purchasers in field visits. In arranging the visits the consultant made it clear that she wanted advice and guidance rather than cash. In return, the agency received some very useful feedback and advice which it used in designing its approaches to authorities.

Do some basic market research

The term 'marketing' often confuses people: it is wrongly seen as entirely about selling. Understanding the market in which you intend to operate is key.

- **Understanding how the market for the project operates**
  How are decisions about resources made? How do other players in the market operate? What is the economic position of the market? Is spending likely to go up or down?

- **Determining how the project can fit best in the market**
  What will the project do differently? Where should it focus its resources?

- **Deciding how best to enter the market**
  How can it best be launched? Who are the key opinion formers? What would persuade and influence them to work with you?

- **Deciding how best to stay in the market**
  What do we need to do to keep and improve our position?

- **Build interest and relationships first**
  All too often, new projects use a cold calling approach – they ask direct for funding without building relationships. A key part of the marketing strategy should be about how to inform, interest and involve potential backers. This might include testing your ideas on potential backers, asking for help, involving them in consultation on the project outline and listening carefully to how the project can work best with them.

- **Recognise lead-times**
  In most instances, the time involved in introducing the project, developing interest, processing a funding application and getting a decision is underestimated. In the public sector the budget setting process is practically a year-round activity. A new project has to win support from officers and political backing, identify from where funds can be taken, go through a several-stage priority bidding process and then be approved in a formal process. Early involvement and an understanding of the stages involved makes good sense.

- **Make links**
  Few backers are prepared to give money away these days without anticipating some kind of direct or indirect connection. The funding strategy needs to identify what kinds of mutual interest or need the project can satisfy. Possible interests may include advancing a policy or social interest, extending learning or making an impact. Be sure to speak the same language as your backers.

Building your case

Funding and commissioning bodies have their own language and terminology, and often these terms can be confusing and block communication. Here are some of the main tools and processes used, particularly by government and public sector agencies.

Tool or process	Description	Purpose
Business case	A business case sets out the economic, organisational and overall benefits involved in a new project.	It should show how the project fits with the funder's published strategy or goals.
Business plan	A written plan setting out the background, goals, strategy, financial and resource details of the organisation for the immediate future. The business plan makes the case for the organisation by setting out its strategy, intended activities and management arrangements. A business plan can last anywhere between one to five years.	The business plan should show that the host organisation has a clear strategy, has been diligent in planning and organising itself and is capable of running the project.
Delivery plan	A statement of targeted outputs and outcomes that a project should achieve.	Often required by government agencies to show how the project will deliver the various outputs that make up the project.
Evaluation	This looks at either the project's process (how it works) or the project's programme (what it delivers) to assess whether it meets its original goals and objectives.	It is useful to describe how and when the project will be evaluated.
Exit strategy	A plan of what will happen at the end of the project and how the project will close down – sometimes called the succession plan or legacy plan.	A good exit strategy ensures that a project can close in an ordered way. It also ensures that the work of the project is carried forward and sustained.
Milestones	Key events marking a clear stage in completing a main stage of the project. Often the term 'landmark' is used instead.	If the overall aim of the project is a large or long-term one, it is useful to have milestones to break it down and make it more manageable.
Performance measurement	Preset measures or indicators by which the outputs and outcomes of the project will be measured.	Shows how the project's progress will be monitored.
Project appraisal	The process of evaluating a proposed project to see if it is worth investing in.	The project appraisal process should set out the specific criteria by which requests for support should be evaluated.
Quality assurance	Evidence of clear minimum standards showing the minimum levels of service and practice that should operate.	Good quality assurance systems should ensure that users should be able to expect a consistent level of service.
Targets	Preset outputs or outcomes that the project should aim to meet.	A statement of what the funder or commissioner expects the project to be able to deliver.

The following concepts can be very useful in making the case for investment in a new project.

Term	Description	Example
Added value	A term used to show how initial investment is enhanced or added to by what the project does with it.	A government scheme may provide funds of £30,000 for a project managed by a local agency. The agency uses volunteers, local contacts and expertise to deliver the project. These factors 'add value' to the original £30,000. It is possible to suggest an equivalent cash value of the added value factors.
Additionality	Similar to added value, but usually referring to adding extra income. Initial funding of a project may be regarded as pump-priming, which aims to bring in other resources.	A project is able to use its initial investment to bring in extra resources.
Floor targets	A generic term used by government to describe targets that set a minimum standard for disadvantaged groups or areas, or a narrowing of the gap between them and the rest of the country.	A project is able to show how it might aid meeting the relevant floor target in an area such as literacy and numeracy targets in schools.
Impact	What difference the project is able to make.	A project produced an impact analysis setting out the short and longer-term gains of its work.
Inputs	The resources (finance, equipment and other resources) directed into a project.	A project is awarded a grant of £45,000 to deliver a service.
Leverage	The process by which the project brings in other money.	A project was able to add extra resources to the ones provided by the sponsor.
Match funding	A funder agrees to part-fund a project on the basis that another funder also will contribute.	Two charitable foundations agreed to share the risk and both contribute 50% towards the cost of a new project.
Outputs	What the project produces and delivers. Outputs are usually physical or measurable items.	An information service might be open for 25 hours a week, see 74 clients and open 42 cases.
Outcomes	The benefits and overall difference that the project makes.	Outcomes for an information service might include how being better informed has improved users' circumstances and increased their knowledge and opportunities.
Sustainable benefits	Evidence that the longer-term impact and effect of the project has been thought about. Once a sustainable project has ended, other things (services, activities and relationships) should be able to continue.	Through doing a three-year follow-up, a housing project was able to demonstrate that many of the young homeless people whom it had rehoused had gone on to education and employment.

Term	Description	Example
Synergy	How projects work together, avoid duplication of effort and create partnerships.	An organisation argued that having an advice project, education project and a health project all operating in the same building provided synergy, as users might come in to access one service and then go on to another.
Value for money	A study of a project to check that the inputs are planned on a sound economic base, that the outputs are efficiently managed and that the outcomes are worthwhile and effective in meeting the original purpose or need.	An alternative to custody project demonstrated that its operating costs were low, that it was well used and well organised, and that a higher proportion of its clients stopped offending than those referred to other alternatives.
Vision statement	A broad statement of the overall goals and values that underpin the project.	An organisation working to increase educational opportunities was able to show that all of its projects were linked together by a commitment to work with hard-to-reach groups and a belief that education was key to turning around people's lives.

It is important to be clear about the kind of relationship that potential backers want and need. Four types of relationships are possible:

- funder or supporter
- client or purchaser
- collaborator
- investor.

Role	Relationship
Funder or supporter	Donor – gives money (usually as a grant) to support a project
Client or purchaser	A contractual one – an agreement is formed whereby the project will deliver certain outputs or achieve set outcomes
Collaborator	A partnership – working together to achieve a shared goal
Investor	A long-term relationship to tackle a problem or achieve a specific outcome

All of these relationships need different kinds of relationship building and approaches. There may be some considerable overlap.

Maintain the relationship

Many commercial businesses make the mistake of pursuing new business rather than consolidating and maintaining their existing customer base. Obtaining new business is expensive and time-consuming compared with keeping what you have already. A key part of a funding strategy is to establish how to maintain and consolidate existing relationships by involving, communicating and working with existing backers. They should be seen as long-term investors, rather than completed sales.

Ways to build support for a new project

Here are some practical ideas on how to gain support from potential sponsors.

1 Make connections

Often it is necessary to invest in building relationships and raising your profile in the hope that it will lead to resources. The manager of a youth development agency described how attending partnership meetings, inter-agency events and other networking occasions directly led to being invited to manage a project supporting vulnerable young people:

> *All that work, which at the time sometimes felt pointless, raised our profile and meant that they felt confident about working with us.*

2 Start at the outcomes

Start at the end rather than the means. For example, a minibus is a means to an end. However, improving the ability of an isolated community to get access to services and jobs is an end or an outcome. Start at the outcome (that is, what the project aims to achieve) and then work back to how it will be done (that is, what outputs and services).

3 Start early

Organisations can have long lead-times for making decisions and committing resources. As the manager of an alcohol and drugs agency commented:

> *It took nearly a year to get key people to identify the need and understand our idea for a particular project, and then a further six months to find the resources to do it.*

4 Link up with key priorities

Particularly in the public sector it is useful to identify how a planned project links in with published strategies. Being able to link a project into things such as local area agreements, commissioning strategies and service plans can help the process.

5 Identify and minimise risks

As outlined previously, it is useful to show that you have considered what can go wrong. A simple risk analysis showing that you have identified potential risks, have taken steps to prevent them and have contingencies in place, should they happen, shows that the project has been diligent and thorough.

6 Develop pilots

A pilot project usually involves trying the project out on a smaller basis to establish if it works. Being able to show potential backers the pilot in operation or an evaluation of a pilot can be a very powerful way of making the case for a bigger project.

7 Bring in partners

Sponsors tend to feel safety in numbers. Being able to show that other agencies have agreed to back the project might be a way of encouraging a sponsor to commit. This can lead to a match-funding arrangement.

8 Ask for advice

Asking potential sponsors for their view on how a project plan could be developed can pay off, as they may be able to give advice as to how a project could be presented. If a potential sponsor rejects a project bid, it is worthwhile asking for feedback. Such feedback might provide useful information, and even open up a conversation as to how future projects can be developed.

A business case

Increasingly, organisations are using the term 'business case' and are requiring the people bidding for projects to produce a business case to support any request for investment in a new project. At its simplest, the business case must make the argument for backing a new initiative and show how the project will make a valuable return. The Office of Government Commerce suggests that there are five key elements to a business case:

- strategic fit
- options appraisal
- commercial aspects
- affordability
- achievability.

Strategic fit

The business case needs to show how the proposed project fits with key strategies and objectives. For example, an organisation bidding to a health commissioner would need to demonstrate that its project is aligned with the commissioner's published strategy and priorities.

Options appraisal

The business case should outline briefly the other options that were considered in developing the project proposal. A useful way of summarisng this is through a simple cost–benefit matrix. It might be useful to include a 'do nothing' alternative in the options appraisal, in order to highlight the need to act.

Commercial aspects

This area is applicable only to programmes that might involve some external commercial funding, such as a joint venture with a private company.

Affordability

This is an outline of ballpark estimates of the projected whole-life cost of the project. It might be useful in this section to explain the business model behind the project: that is, the funding mix.

Achievability

In this area the case needs to outline in broad terms the overall plan, key milestones, significant risks (and how to avoid or manage them) and brief evidence that the bidding organisation has the skills and experience to deliver the project.

CASE STUDY

The long decision

In one fairly typical (and reasonably well-managed) local authority, a national charity submitted a proposal to run a small project costing the authority £18,000. There was strong support within the authority for the project – indeed, the agency had been encouraged by a senior manager to put forward a bid.

The timetable from early discussions to project agreement was more than 18 months. In outline here is the chain of events.

January: Meetings with senior manager and chair and vice chair of the relevant service committee to discuss the project. Councillors and the assistant director visit a similar project and are very impressed. There is no chance of funding until the next financial year, as decisions on available funding have been made already.

Late February: Urgent activity. A possibility that the department may have underspent in one area this year. The chance that the project could be started on this underspend was explored, but failed to materialise.

April: New financial year.

May: Council annual general meeting appoints new committee chairs. There is a meeting with the departmental assistant director to see if the project could be included in a package of projects being developed as part of a bid for a newly-created central government regeneration initiative. The possibility of funding the project from the National Lottery is raised and dismissed.

June: The project will not go into the government regeneration initiative, as it does not fit the current criteria. The departmental director briefs the new chair and vice chair about the departmental strategic plan. The project is identified as being a medium to high priority. Over the summer months reports are circulated that the council is likely to have to make up to five per cent savings in all service areas.

September: The charity is invited to contribute to a short training session for relevant departmental staff on the experience of the project elsewhere. The response is good. A meeting with the assistant director is positive. The project will go forward as one of the department's main bids.

October: A cabinet meeting of the key councillors in the controlling party reviews future plans and is prepared to back the plan, provided that officers find a way to reallocate current spending.

November: The charity is asked to prepare and present a business plan to council officers. There is detailed discussion about costings, service plans and how the project fits with the department's priorities and existing services.

January: There are positive indications from an assistant director that there may be some space in the budget following a reorganisation.

February: The charity makes a short presentation to the council subcommittee. The spending proposal is discussed in the controlling political group and policy and resources committee. The charity is asked to produce a scaled-down project as a contingency measure.

March: The council budget is approved, including a slightly reduced budget for the project. There are negotiations with officers on the service contract between the charity and the council.

Three points are worth noting about this process.

1   The charity spent most of its time building a relationship from which funding for a project would develop. It did not see the issue as simply about fundraising.

2   The internal process within the authority was complex. Power was shared between several different parties. The charity needed to find out how decisions were made and how influence could be exercised best – the time spent doing this was worthwhile. It needed to find a key player, in this case an assistant director who advised and guided the charity through the process.

3   The process took time. On more than one occasion the charity thought that the project would not happen. It had to alter its own timescales continually and be prepared to change to some extent the design of the project to fit with the authority's interests. Managing this was particularly hard, as the charity was concerned that it could lose the distinctiveness of the project.

Planning and costing a project

This chapter introduces a range of practical techniques which can be used to plan out and cost a project. Costing and planning a project should be more than a bureaucratic chore: done properly, it gives a focus to the project and can help newly-appointed project workers to understand their role and what they need to deliver.

About planning

Approaches to planning range from almost being a project in itself, as complex project plans are drawn up with detailed targets and schedules, to projects that manage to operate with little deliberate or formal plans.

As one experienced project worker put it:

In most of our projects we get by with little structure: things turn up unexpectedly, opportunities arise and, in people-based projects, things rarely happen to schedule. We have to be flexible and responsive. We have looked at using traditional planning techniques, but I am worried that we would spend too much time writing plans that could become a straitjacket for the project.

A good plan should be something that adds to the project. It should help those responsible for delivering the project to organise their work and ensure that everything happens in a logical and rational way. In addition, it should be useful in helping to explain the project's intended work to external stakeholders, such as funders and partners.

A good project plan needs to be able to:

- identify and set out all the tasks and decisions involved in the project in a clear and measurable way
- match human and other resources available with the work involved
- enable monitoring of the project so progress can be acknowledged
- highlight any departure from the plan at an early stage, so that remedial action can be taken quickly to overcome delays, blocks or problems
- produce key milestones to which those involved in the project can work.

A simple planning framework is based around three key elements:

1 starting at the end point and working backwards
2 identifying key milestones towards the end-points
3 scheduling in and resourcing tasks and decisions to achieve each milestone.

Established project planning techniques

Project management as a branch of management studies has its main roots in the defence and engineering industries. Several techniques and systems have been drawn up to manage and plan complex projects. They all contain the following elements:

- listing and estimating all the activities involved in a project
- noting any dependent relationship between activities (e.g. activity x can only happen after activity y has been completed)
- getting all the activities into a logical order
- calculating the shortest time to get through all of the activities in a logical fashion.

The main techniques are as follows.

Critical path model

A critical path is a method of calculating the total duration of all the tasks involved in a project by estimating each task, linking it to others and working out the optimum route (the critical path) through from start to finish.

Programme Evaluation Review Technique

The Programme Evaluation Review Technique (PERT) was developed in the 1950s by the United States Navy to schedule large projects. Similar to a critical path analysis, a PERT chart (sometimes called a network diagram) sets out in graphic form the relationships between tasks and the overall likely duration.

Gantt chart

A Gantt chart (named after Henry L. Gantt) sets out different tasks on a bar chart across a timescale. The strength of a Gantt chart is in its graphic representation and the ability to track progress quickly.

Projects In Controlled Environments

Projects In Controlled Environments (PRINCE) is a process-based method for project management. It is used extensively in UK government and in designing and managing complex projects. PRINCE is based on dividing the project into manageable and controllable stages.

There are several computer software packages, most notably Microsoft Project, use these techniques.

These techniques have a mixed reputation. They provide useful discipline and can help to get things in order and identify potential problems or delays. However, there is a tendency for them to become over-complex and jargonistic. To use the technique properly, all the details about timescales, deadlines and availability need to be available at the start of the project. There is also a tendency for planners to assume that everything works in a logical fashion.

All plans and planning tools need to be active and flexible: they should not be regarded as shackles that tie down the development of the project. Plans need to be reviewed and reshaped in the light of experience and developments, and effective and regular monitoring of the plan is vital.

A useful starting point in developing a project plan is to do a work breakdown schedule: this involves identifying and recording all the different tasks and activities involved in the project. The process of drawing up a work breakdown schedule can be a valuable exercise – it is a useful way of checking that all the different tasks involved in the project are understood and have been identified. Once all the tasks have been identified, time estimates can be allocated to each task. Then the tasks can be linked by spotting dependency relationships (that is, x needs to happen before y). Once the relationships have been identified, the project can be planned using a start-to-finish line.

A useful spin-off from using these techniques is that the planning process can help the people in the project to analyse what is involved in delivering it. For example, the manager of a project set up to design and open a community centre for young people described her experience.

> *At our second project meeting I got the team to list all the work involved in the project. We then pasted them onto a timeline by working out in what order things needed to happen. At the end of the session we had a project plan. The process we used helped people to understand the work involved in different elements of the project. We had a*

useful discussion where we looked at each task and checked that we had the right skills within the team to do it. People could also see how their contribution would fit in with the overall success of the project delivery.

Using milestones to plan

A simpler way of planning a project is to identify the milestones involved in running it. A milestone is the end of one stage or element of the project, then the project can go on to the next phase. Reaching a milestone signals that the project is on track.

In the planning stage it is useful to identify the key milestones to use to measure progress. For example, the steering group of a local children's charity identified five key milestones to achieve its goal of setting up a family centre:

1   appointed trustees, applied for charity registration and started fundraising

2   appointed management group, consultants and freelance fundraiser

3   achieved income commitments up to £55,000

4   leased building and started to advertise for staff

5   agreed open date and planned launch.

The time between each milestone varied considerably. As the chair of the trustees described:

The milestones gave a discipline to our work. They provided a focus to our activity and stopped us galloping ahead. At each milestone the trustees reviewed progress and made sure that we were in a fit state to move onto the next set of tasks.

Milestones work best if they are linked to the completion of key tasks. The milestone should be based on the completion of one phase of the project's life rather than a date set at random, although it is useful to agree an anticipated date when you expect a milestone to be achieved. On reaching a milestone, the following should happen.

■ **Progress is reviewed**
Achieving the milestone shows that you are making progress. It is useful to spend time assessing the work done so far, in order to establish what works and what does not, and to identify any learning points.

■ **The project definition is revisited**
In reaching the milestone you may have learned something that changes the original assumptions and thinking behind the project definition. Is the original plan still sound? Are the success criteria still attainable? What changes might be necessary in the way you envisage the project working?

■ **The detail for the next stage is agreed**
The milestone review should be a useful opportunity to agree the who, what, when and how of the next stage of the project's start-up. Plans should be drawn up which will take the project to the next milestone.

■ **Progress is monitored and celebrated**
Many of us have a problem acknowledging the work that people have contributed: the milestone is a good place to recognise this and to thank them for their contribution. Milestones are commonplace in some industries: for example, in the building trade, when the last brick or beam is put in place, a milestone called 'topping out' is reached and the construction workers drink a toast. This acknowledges the work so far completed and gives people a feeling of making headway. Milestones can help to build up momentum in a project.

Three ways of using milestones

A regeneration project carries out a user consultation event at each milestone:

We ask local people for their opinions and try to get their feedback. It is useful to see consultation not as something you only do at the start in order to get the money. It really should be a continual process.

A crime reduction project uses the milestones to check that all the original partners are still committed and on board:

We use it to check that they have not become passive or sleeping partners – on some occasions it can be a good way of revitalising their commitment to, and involvement in, the project.

An environmental project uses the milestones to check and update the original project plan:

Sometimes it is simply a case of checking that we are on track. In other cases we might need to adjust or reorganise the plan. The milestone is a good point to go back to the project plan.

CASE STUDY

A voluntary organisation used project planning techniques to plan out a limited 12-month project to gather information on, and provide support work to, self-help groups working in a particular locality. The organisation needed a plan to ensure that the project could:

- be started on time
- survey current provision
- produce a paper and web-based directory of current provision
- carry out support work with around six groups
- produce a training pack to carry on the project's work
- organise an event to share practice and close the project.

The first task was to do a work breakdown schedule that identified all the main tasks and activities involved in delivering the project. The project team identified 14 key stages and tasks:

1   project staff in post

2   set up and open project office (1 week)

3   induction of project staff (1 week)

4   consultation with key partners (2 weeks)

5   project launch (1 week)

6   survey current provision (4 weeks)

7   produce website (3 weeks)

8   produce directory (4 weeks)

9   carry out support work (24 weeks)

10   produce training pack (3 weeks)

11   carry out project evaluation (4 weeks)

12   organise closure event (3 weeks)

13   organise and run closure event (4 weeks)

14   close the project (2 weeks).

From the above list, it was possible to identify various project dependencies:

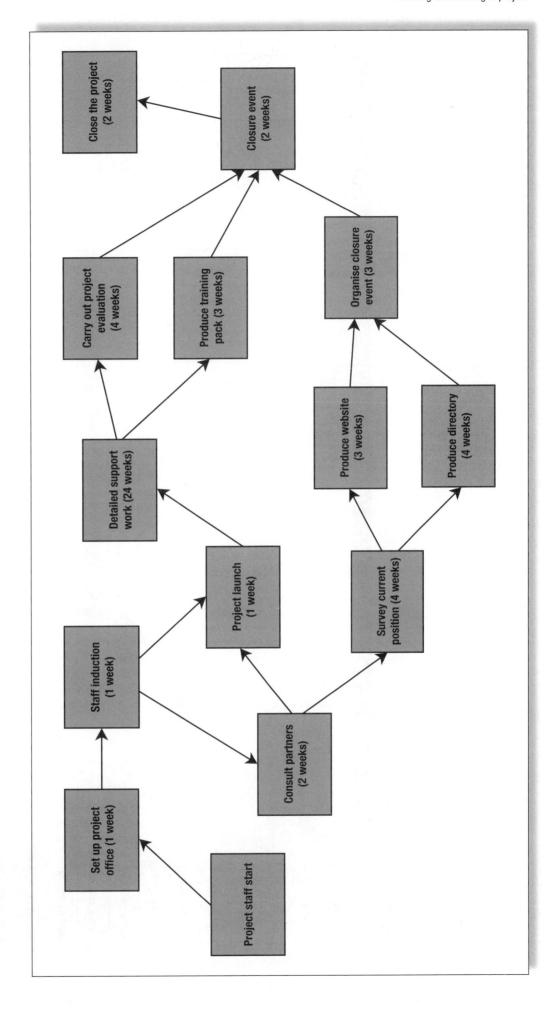

The plan as a Gantt chart

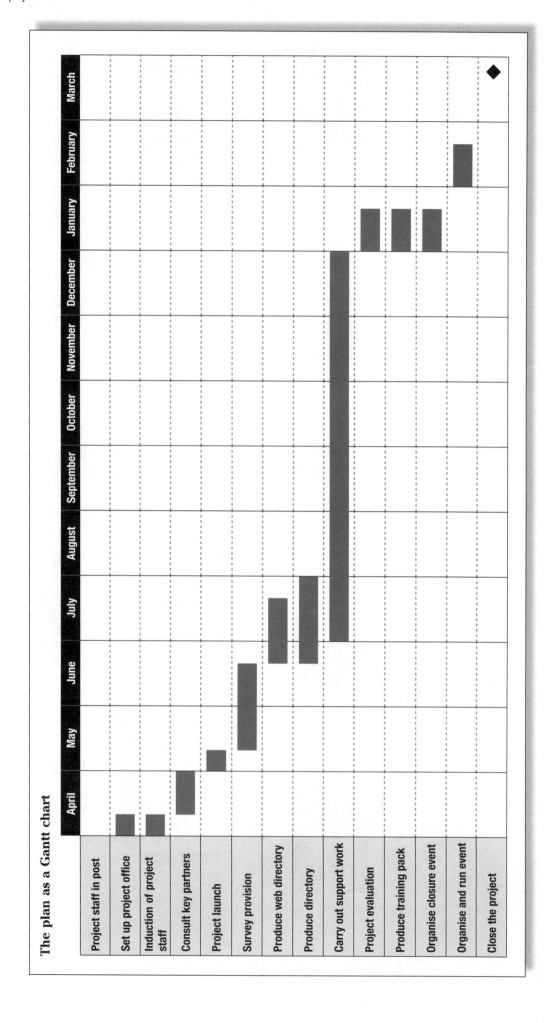

Costing the project

Costing a project involves more than simply throwing a budget together. It involves analysing the structure of the project and the work involved and estimating the associated costs. In the voluntary sector projects have often been undercosted: sometimes this is because project developers believe that a cheap project will find it easier to attract funds, or because the full cost of operating is either not known or not explored fully. Costing requires thorough work; failing to identify costs, or not including the full cost, can create major problems for the project.

There are three ways of dividing up the costs involved in a project:

1 costs that are recurring or non-recurring
2 costs that are fixed or variable
3 costs that are related directly to the project or are an indirect overhead.

Recurring and non-recurring costs

Recurring costs are costs that are expected to be incurred every year as part of the regular cycle of the project. The amount may vary, but the heading will be there every year. Non-recurring costs are one-off costs: these are items that are not anticipated to be paid for every year. Projects often incur two kinds of non-recurring costs: capital costs and costs involved with start-up or closure.

Capital costs

Capital costs are expenditure on items which are not expected to be incurred every year. Central and local government usually organise capital funding separately from annual revenue funding. Some capital items lose value over time: this is called depreciation. With capital items, you need to calculate for how many years you think the capital item will last, and divide this by the total cost – this gives a depreciation rate. For example, a car may cost £10,000, and it is estimated to last for five years. The car depreciates in value by £2,000 every year. If you are going to need a car permanently, you need to plan how you will build up a fund to meet this capital expenditure in five years. Capital items also need repair and eventual replacement, so the purchase of capital items usually leads to annual expenditure on running costs and maintenance. Examples of capital expenditure include buildings and major equipment purchase.

Start-up and closure costs

Invariably, a new project will incur some costs that are one-off items of expenditure because the project is new. These include the costs of the start-up phase and the costs involved in launching a new organisation. Often there are one-off costs associated with making a fixed-term closure, which could include staff redundancies, the costs involved in running down services and producing the end-of-project evaluation. These costs should not be recurring ones and need to be budgeted and accounted for separately.

Fixed or variable costs

Fixed costs are costs that are incurred regardless of how busy the project is. Variable costs relate directly to usage. For example, a transport service will have to pay costs such as permanent staff wages, office rent and hire purchase on vehicles whether it makes one journey or a hundred journeys a month, as these costs are fixed. Costs such as fuel and sessional staff are variable items. The project incurs these costs in direct relation to how busy it is.

The relationship between fixed and variable costs is particularly important in estimating a break-even point for projects that charge for their work. The break-even point is the point at which the project has enough business to achieve an income sufficient to cover its costs.

Current business thinking is to design organisations to be as flexible and economical as possible by increasing the variable element through using sessional rather than permanent staff, and buying in services from external suppliers when needed rather than having them permanently in the organisation. The long-term effects and benefits of this strategy are not clear as yet. It could be that that the increased use of variable items may be more costly and reduces morale within an organisation.

Costs that are directly related to the project or are an indirect overhead

In simple terms, all activities have a direct and an indirect cost. The direct costs are the costs involved in doing the work and delivering the service to the user. Indirect costs are the costs of supporting, managing and running the organisation that hosts and supports the project.

The issue of direct and indirect costs has been a contentious one. Many funding bodies have been quite willing to pay for direct costs, but have refused to pay for indirect costs (or core costs, as they are sometimes known). This has led to organisations having to find other resources to pay for administrative and infrastructure costs, or failing to develop the management and organisational structures necessary to support projects.

Full Cost Recovery model

The Association of Chief Executives of Voluntary Organisations (ACEVO) developed a model to enable organisations to identify all of the costs involved in an activity or project. This model, Full Cost Recovery (ACEVO, 2001), is designed to ensure that the fee for a service or project reflects the full costs of delivery, including a fair contribution to the organisation's overhead costs. At the policy level, central government has backed the principles of full cost recovery. The Treasury review of the voluntary sector in public service delivery said:

> *Funders should recognise that it is legitimate for providers to include the relevant element of overheads in their cost estimates for providing a given service under service agreement or contract. (ACEVO, 2001)*

The ACEVO model identifies four types of organisational costs:

Category	Definition	Examples
1 Project output costs	The direct costs of delivering the project.	The project worker's employment costs. Materials and resources used in delivering the project.
2 Project support costs	Costs involved in providing support to the project.	Costs of supervision, support and back-up to the project.
3 Organisational indirect costs	The cost of various organisational functions that do not directly link to service delivery.	Costs of some central functions, e.g. human resources, accounting.
4 Strategic and developmental costs	The organisational cost involved in policy work, external representation and developing the organisation.	Cost of staff time involved in external policy work, networking and research and development.

In outline terms, the process of implementing full cost recovery involves four stages.

1 Deciding how to divide up the organisation's costs

This involves deciding which cost of activity centres to use. This could be by:

- project
- type of user
- geography
- funding or income stream.

2 Allocating direct costs

Once the cost centres have been agreed, the direct costs can be allocated to each activity. The direct costs are the costs that are dedicated to delivering a particular activity. So, for example, in an advice project, the direct costs would include the cost of employing an advice worker and the costs of any materials and resources used by the project to deliver the outputs. Some resources might be shared across several centres: for example, an outreach worker might spend half of their time on community development work, a quarter on the youth project, and a quarter on the advice project. So, a quarter of their employment costs would be allocated to the advice project.

3 Allocating indirect overheads

Usually the indirect costs are all the other costs which cannot be allocated as a direct cost to a project or service. Indirect costs cover the things that are needed to run the organisation properly and provide support to the projects. In the past, indirect costs have been divided out among the cost centres. So, for example, an agency running six projects might establish that its indirect costs are £87,000. This figure is shared among the six projects, so each project would be charged £14,500 as a management or overhead charge. Although this is simple to do, it is somewhat arbitrary; it might be more useful to look at how much of the overhead each project actually uses.

4 Analysis

Once the full cost of all projects has been established, they can be combined to produce a full organisational budget. As a final stage, all of the costs can be compiled into a budget for the whole organisation. At this point it is useful to compare the full cost of the project with what the organisation is being paid (if by a commissioner) or funded for it. In developing this approach to costing, three things often happen.

- **The cost of the project is more than expected**
  This can happen because it is the first time that the full costs have been identified, and may suggest that in the past, the full cost of operating a project has been underestimated. In some organisations the gap between the actual full cost of the project and what the organisation has been paid to do it has been significant. This has highlighted the extent to which organisations have subsidised projects (sometimes without knowing) and lacked useful financial information.

- **Costs need to be justified**
  This process often causes a power shift in organisations, as people start to question whether the amount paid in indirect costs is reasonable. Does central management really add value to the project, or does the project have to carry a top-heavy bureaucracy?

- **The way costs are allocated can be arbitrary**
  There are no strict rules about what is a direct, shared or indirect cost. For example, one agency ran five local projects. The agency coordinator felt that it was not right to regard all of her salary as an indirect cost. Instead, she reviewed her time and came up with a breakdown of 40% of her time on the agency-wide issues (an indirect cost), 30% providing support and supervision to the projects (project support costs), and 30% split

between two projects doing direct service delivery work (direct costs charged to the two projects).

Understanding the financial structure of the project

As well as working out the likely costs of the project and sources of expenditure, thought needs to be given to the financial structure or business model that underpins the project. Four factors are important here:

1   the movement of money within the project

2   patterns of cashflow

3   pricing policies for projects which earn money

4   the need for sensible contingency funds.

It is quite possible for a budget to balance but for the finances of the project to remain problematic. This is not just about the 'bottom line'. In setting up a project, it is worth exploring the following potential issues.

Start-up costs subsidise the first year

Often, enthusiasm for a new project means that funders can be quite generous at the beginning and provide money for the start-up. This is fine, provided that the project does not rely upon start-up money in the first year to subsidise its running costs. For example, one small project with a total income of £60,000 received a one-off start-up budget of £12,000 in its first year. Often, the start-up budget was used for items which were of a recurring nature, and this created serious financial problems in the second and third years.

Is the balance of costs right?

Is the balance between restricted and non-restricted income right? How do you make sure that all costs can be met? Can you justify the amounts paid in management and administration? There is no fixed rule as to what an appropriate ratio is between direct project costs and expenditure on organisational management. Some organisations aim to keep management costs to about 15 to 20% of the project's total costs. However, it is possible to make useful comparisons between projects only if the same rules have been followed as to what direct costs, support costs and indirect costs are.

Are there any time-lag problems?

Could a slow or a delayed start affect the project's income? It is usual for project expenditure to be high at the start of the project. Could this cause a cashflow problem?

How and when will we have to replace capital items?

How long will our capital items really last for? When do we need to replace them? How can we set aside a fund to do this?

Will there be sufficient uncommitted working capital?

Is there sufficient flexibility in the budget? Will we be able to follow up opportunities and use our cash intelligently?

Project papers

Sample project structure and plan

Use this document to outline the main organisational aspects of the project:

■ the key roles and relationships involved
■ the project's outline plan
■ how the project will be monitored.

A project to recruit young volunteers

Project sponsor	Project manager and time commitment
The management committee	Full-time project worker – fixed-term contract
Other staff input into this project	**How will the project be managed**
Other team members will be expected to support and work with the project as part of their normal duties	Project worker will be line-managed by director Possibility of a project steering group to develop the project

The project plan

Project milestone	Estimated date	Key measures at this milestone
Project operational	Within four weeks of the project starting	Office open, staff in post On budget
Campaign plan agreed after consultation with sector	Within eight weeks of the project starting	Number of groups and young people consulted Plan agreed
Public volunteer recruitment campaign launched	At the end of quarter 1	Number of participating and volunteers recruited
Best practice consultancies with six groups carried out	By the end of September	Feedback from groups
Young volunteers event	November	Numbers participating Media coverage
Plan for years 2 and 3 agreed	By the end of January	Plan agreed

Delegation to project manager

Organisation of the project

Delivery of the project plan

Spend up to £200 in line with budget

Able to speak on behalf of the project to external groups and media

Project monitoring arrangements

Monthly monitoring report

Six-monthly review event scheduled to revisit project definition and plan

End of first year evaluation exercise to be carried out to review progress and identify 'early outcomes'

Project papers

Sample project milestone report

Use this document at each project milestone.

Milestone	Best practice consultancies with six groups carried out

What has been achieved?
Six consultancies carried out
Four groups have developed action plans to develop recruitment campaigns targeted at young people
One group requesting further help

Is the project on track?
Yes – milestone completed by the end of September as estimated

Identify any significant blocks or problems that the project is experiencing	Identify any changes to the project's original plan
Organising the consultancies took longer than expected in two groups One group unable to develop action plan due to staff changes	No significant change

Note any particular action needed at this milestone
Follow-up contact with the groups will be needed

Next milestone	Original estimate	Comments
Young volunteers event	November	Event planned for 18 November

Comments on work needed to get to next milestone
Detailed plan has been drawn up

Getting it organised

The **starting phase** of a project is usually hectic. Detailed design and organisational decisions need to be made that will shape the project and influence its success. This chapter looks at five issues:

1 what needs to be different about how we manage projects
2 the project's structure
3 staffing the project
4 working with partnerships
5 planning the project launch.

Often, projects are not designed; rather, they are thrown together to meet fast-approaching deadlines. Four features make the design of projects important and different from how organisations have been established and managed traditionally:

1 projects need to be designed for organisational flexibility rather than permanence
2 projects need structures and ways of working that streamline and are simple
3 projects usually need to fit in with the host organisation
4 most projects are fixed term – there is a clear point in the future when the project will end.

Most of today's organisations were designed to be permanent rather than carry out short-term or project-based work. They were intended to minimise change and allow for command and control from the top down: they worked fairly well, provided that little changed. They provided continuity, certainty and control. There are three key principles of traditional organisational design.

- **A clear hierarchical structure**
  Policymaking and strategy is carried out at the top, and service delivery is at the bottom. Some think and others act. Often, the number of levels or compartments in a structure grow rapidly, and very tight spans of control are created. The more contact there is with the user, the fewer the rewards. Resources such as finance are held centrally and tightly controlled.

- **Tight boundaries**
  Most organisations use departmental, professional or geographic divides as the key organisational building blocks: a person knows their job and sticks to it. This often creates tension within the organisation, as different groups clash and play out office politics, or work falls between two places.

- **Top-down communication**
  Little formal communication goes back up and across the organisation. There is little feedback or real dialogue. There is often poor communication between teams and functions..

In this scenario, narrow job design, strict boundaries and top-heavy structures made change, teamwork and flexibility difficult. Traditional thinking about management also produced a fragmented organisation in which few people saw the whole picture: instead, people only saw their bit of it.

Projects need to be designed with the following features in mind.

- **People and resources must be used flexibly within the project to meet its end result**
  The project needs to be geared up to meet its tasks rather than simply exist within the structure. Projects need to be about performance and delivery. They need to be outward-facing.

- **Everyone in the project must see the big picture**
  Projects usually have very flat structures so everyone can keep in touch and feel part of the project. Everyone involved must feel committed to the whole of the project, rather than just their part of it.

- **The project's structure must enable it to change as required**
  Projects go through different phases. The kind of work needed in the start-up phase will be different from work needed in the main part of the project, or at its end. Staff roles and responsibilities need to be adaptable. Many aspects of the project will be temporary rather than fixed.

- **Teamwork as a building block**
  In smaller projects, staff need to be flexible in how they operate and often work without much direct supervision. Projects need to consider recruiting people who are experienced in being part of a team, are able to cover for and support other team members, and possibly can become multi-skilled.

- **Strategy versus structure**
  There are not many established rules on how to design projects. The structures and systems we have can restrict and limit the strategy that the host organisation can follow.

Badly designed job descriptions, staff structures and other systems can get in the way of the project. For example, a director of a specialist advice agency described his experience of this issue:

> When we set up the project we made very quick decisions about what sort of jobs we would need. We recruited people for their particular technical competence. We started out with three individuals who were experts in their own fields. However, the project's plan requires them to take on pieces of work that require a broad range of skills. Often they have to work as trainers or local advisers and operate outside of their specialist boundary. The job roles that we agreed and recruited for have created a structure that works against our strategy.

Structural and system factors such as job roles, reporting relationships, budget and resource controls, and even factors such as office layouts, all have a major impact on how we work. Therefore, they need to be designed after the overall strategic direction and priorities for the project have been agreed. Structures and systems need to fit the project, rather than the project having to fit in with existing structures and systems.

Developing the project's structure

When we design a new project, we are inclined to copy the way in which large and established organisations work. For example, a new campaign group was set up by a group of activists who mainly worked in large public sector organisations. They drafted a project structure which had a committee structure reflecting their experience of working in a large organisation. The staff team spent most of its first year struggling to service organisational bureaucracy and controls. The new campaign director had to fight hard to persuade them to reduce the number of meetings and standing subcommittees from six to two, renegotiate staff job descriptions to include flexibility as a main task, and reduce the amount of paper reports required.

The following eight points are useful in building a flexible project structure.

1 Make delegation of responsibilities and decision-making explicit

Lines of responsibility are rarely made clear. The boundary of what you can do, how much money you can spend or what decisions you can make only become clear once you step over them. It is easier to agree and review boundaries in advance rather than after a problem. Good delegation should include tasks (that is, what work you have to do) and what decisions you can make. Some organisations are very good at delegating (or even dumping) work, but not so good at delegating decision-making power.

2 Keep the remit of committees focused

The remit and responsibilities of project boards or steering groups need to be agreed and documented. People need to be clear about what decisions need to be made by the committee and what information the committee needs to make informed decisions.

3 Watch out for 'democratic overload'

Even in quite small projects, meetings can take over. Subcommittees and working groups are formed to work on an issue or even as a way of pretending to make progress. The need for committees, subgroups and meetings should be looked at regularly: if they are not adding value to the project and simply have become part of an organisational routine, they should be stood down.

4 Budget for flexibility

Projects often need a budgeting system that allows for some flexibility. The project may need to move cash between budget headings to allow for changed patterns of need. The project may need occasional access to funds to develop new work and follow up opportunities. Certainly, in the first year or so, the budget should be able to support reasonable flexibility.

5 Identify relevant performance measures

To monitor the project's work and ensure progress towards the milestones and overall goals measurement is important. The project should agree some simple measures to ensure that it is informed of progress. Be careful not to have too many measures. A few well chosen measures should act as a project's dashboard to help it to steer and alert it to any problems.

6 Use information technology intelligently

Most organisations have computers. However in offices, most computers are grossly underused, the use of technology is not planned, and training and support is not budgeted. Technology is used only to automate what was done previously by hand. The potential of email to aid communication, and databases and other systems to help with other tasks, is overlooked. Viewing technology as a vital part of the project's organisation and planning, and how best to use it from the outset, can be time-saving.

7 Control paperwork

Organisations can drown in paperwork. From the start, encourage people to communicate in Plain English: avoid long reports and unnecessary systems and procedures.

8 Build in periodic organisational reviews

It is useful early on in a project to review how well the organisational systems and structures are helping to achieve the project's strategy. For example, three times a year, one health agency holds a two-hour organisational 'fitness workshop'. Blocks and barriers to effective teamwork, communication and progress are identified and eliminated. Even in a small agency unnecessary systems and bureaucracy can creep up quickly.

Common project design faults

Organisations can create structures for projects that do not work. Here are some examples of common ones.

The one-worker project

When is a project too small to be an effective organisation? The sole employee of a self-help agency described her role as 'project director, fundraiser, ideas person, administrator, editor, office cleaner, bookkeeper and anything else that is thrown at me'. The project worker had so many roles and expectations placed on her that the job was impossible. Everything depended on her. The steering group was committed but lacked the time to give support. Most of the employee's time was spent on keeping the organisation together rather than providing direct services. Often she was isolated, did not feel part of anything and lacked access to any support or supervision.

Rather than becoming a separate project the steering group might have explored ways of locating the project within an existing organisation or contracting out some of the activities. Projects built around one key worker only work if there are considerable support, supervision and review mechanisms built into their structure.

The top-heavy project

As part of a time management course, the three workers of an education project recorded how they actually spent their time in quarter-hour intervals. They were shocked to learn that nearly 60% of their combined time went on servicing the organisation, attending meetings and preparing reports. The project had allowed a system of meetings, committees, reports and other aspects of internal bureaucracy to grow and multiply. It had an organisational structure that was far too big and time-consuming in proportion to the size and work of the project.

Systems and structures are important, but do have a habit of propagating. Meetings take place because they are scheduled rather than needed, long reports look better than shorter ones, and technology provides information that is rarely used, but looks interesting. It is worthwhile to check regularly the balance between the time spent on direct or primary activities and indirect or internal activities. In addition, it is useful to prune administrative systems and processes periodically.

The open-ended job

Job descriptions tend to be written to make sure that every possible activity is included, in order to prevent conflicts. New postholders have to spend the first few months of the project working out exactly what the job is for; vague titles (such as 'development officer') and long lists of possible tasks give little clue as to what is really important in the job and what kind of impact is necessary. All too often, individuals do the part of the job that they like or understand best.

It is important to be clear exactly what is expected of a job. What difference can an individual make? What should their priorities be? How will success be measured? Well-written descriptions, efficient induction and probationary reviews for new workers, regular reviews and work planning can all help to overcome this problem.

The powerless assistant or deputy

As a project expands, it can fail to think about its structure, and simply add to it. A common way of doing this is to give the hard-pressed senior person in the project a deputy or assistant as a way of helping them. A deputy or assistant-type role can only work if certain tasks are clearly delegated to the deputy and they have some autonomy. All too often, deputies and assistants become human 'dumping grounds' for things that their boss no longer wants to do. They lack any independent authority or power, and become an understudy.

Rather than creating a deputy or assistant to a role, it is better to review how tasks and responsibilities can be reallocated among existing staff and, if needed, to create a new post with clear responsibilities and tasks. They may still report to the senior person, but not as a stand-in.

Issue equals job

One national agency has a track record such that whenever it identifies a policy or controversial issue, it creates a job (or if it is a big issue, a whole project) around the issue. Over the past 10 years it has created an equal opportunities project, user involvement officer and, most recently, an environmental issues project. Setting up these projects creates the illusion that the agency is committed to, and making progress on, the issue. However, the reality is different. In all cases, new postholders have to spend time trying to define exactly what is expected of them, and in several cases, by the time they have been appointed, the organisation has lost interest in the issue and moved on to other things.

Good projects and good jobs are task-orientated rather than issue-orientated. There needs to be clarity as to how performance in the job will be measured, what success means and what is expected of the postholder. If these things are unclear, then a new project worker is likely to spend time trying to work out what they should be doing, rather than delivering the project.

Sealed containers in the organisation

A local housing agency grew in traditional pattern. It created jobs and then departments based around the traditional job areas: housing management, maintenance, finance, development and director's office. Very quickly the five departments began to define how they wanted to organise their work. Over time, it became obvious that tenants had to deal with several individuals to get a problem solved. In the old days one person could assess it, plan it and, if not do it themselves, then they could call in a contractor. Nowadays, issues are referred to different departments, which all have their own systems and procedures.

Delays, paperwork and conflicts between departments have increased

As a project grows, it is important to check that the structure and system supports the task rather than becomes an activity in itself. A useful technique is to track all the stages and people involved in a simple service or activity, and to see how it could be simplified or managed better. It is also worthwhile examining how the organisation could be designed around the user and the processes involved in meeting their needs, rather than traditional specialist or professional boundaries.

Staffing the project

Recruiting staff to work on fixed-term projects can be difficult. The fixed-term nature of the project might make it a less attractive option to people in permanent jobs, and the requirements of the project might be too much for one person. Here are some alternatives to directly recruiting staff.

Secondment

It might be possible to offer the project as a secondment opportunity. Under this arrangement, at the end of the project the worker returns to their original job. Often, secondments can provide valuable career and development opportunities for staff that they would not be able to have in their own organisation. It is useful to have a written agreement between the organisations covering responsibilities, supervision arrangements and a process for handling problems.

Interim management

An increasing number of agencies and individual consultants offer interim or locum management. The interim manager works at the project to carry out a specific number of tasks, and usually brings a high level of particular skills and expertise. For example, an arts project used an interim manager to deliver the first part of its project, as the chair of trustees stated:

> *The first phase of the project needed someone with high level computer skills and experience of building works. We were not going to need these skills for the rest of the project; using an interim project manager got the project off to a good start and gave us a real boost.*

Subcontracting

One possibility might be to arrange for another organisation to carry out specific tasks rather than employing someone. This could include providing office and administration support or carrying out a particular task such as event organisation.

Internal secondment

It might be possible to deploy someone from within the organisation to work on the project and recruit someone to cover their time away. It is important that an internal secondee is able to move properly from one role to another – the project will suffer if they are pulled back continually into their substantive role.

All of these possibilities need to be considered and should be based on clear and firm agreements. It is useful to check with the key project funders to see whether they have any view on these approaches.

Employing staff on fixed-term contracts

As mentioned previously, employing staff on a fixed-term basis can be a complicated issue, and organisations should seek proper legal advice. A fixed-term contract is one which lasts for a specified time, is set in advance (for example, a two-year funded project) or ends with the completion of a specified task (for example, when an element of the project has been completed) or when a specified event takes place (for example, a community festival).

Unless there are special circumstances which can be justified, an employer must treat fixed-term employees in the same way as their comparable permanent employees. This could include:

- the same pay and conditions
- the same or equivalent benefits package

- the same or equivalent pension scheme
- the same opportunity to apply for vacancies for permanent posts in the organisation.

Fixed-term employees also have access to the same employment rights as their permanent equivalents. Under the Fixed-term Employees (Prevention of Less Favourable Treatment) Regulations 2002, any employee who has been on a fixed-term contract for four or more years (excluding any period before 10 July 2002) will usually be classed in law as a permanent employee if their contract is renewed, or if they are re-engaged on a new fixed-term contract. There can be exceptions in instances where the employer can objectively justify a renewal or extension of the fixed-term status.

In particular, advice should be taken on how to end a fixed-term contract. There can be circumstances where fixed-term employees can qualify for redundancy payments, or are able to take legal action against their employer if they believe that their contract has been ended unfairly or not renewed. Clauses in letters of appointment or contracts giving up rights to redundancy or to take action are usually regarded as void (unless the employer could objectively justify otherwise).

A partnership-based project

There is an increased trend from government to create partnerships between agencies and across sectors. Many new government initiatives for regeneration, health improvement and education have at their core the development of partnerships between public, private and voluntary sectors. Partnerships can have different roles and scope.

- **Some partnerships are created to bid for money**
  Increasingly, partnerships are assembled to bid to government for funding. The existence of the partnership demonstrates that all of the main relevant interests are behind the bid.
- **Some partnerships are of a strategic nature**
  They commission projects, take an overview of needs and monitor progress.
- **Other partnerships are formed to deliver a project**
  These are practical, and by bringing people from different backgrounds and experience together, the project should be able to achieve more.

Partnership working can bring great benefits. It can draw in different skills, use resources better and begin to break down some of the barriers which often stop effective delivery. However, the good intentions behind partnership working can fail to be carried forward.

CASE STUDY

A project manager for a health improvement project described her partnership project:

It all started well, but soon problems emerged. All of the professionals involved in the partnership – doctors, social workers, home visitors and teachers – spoke a different language and had a very different style of operating. After a few months it became obvious that several people were only involved in the project either to protect their patch or to grab money for their agency. When the programme ran into difficulties, people started to drift away from the project and stopped turning up to meetings.

A structure for partnerships

A common model looks like this:

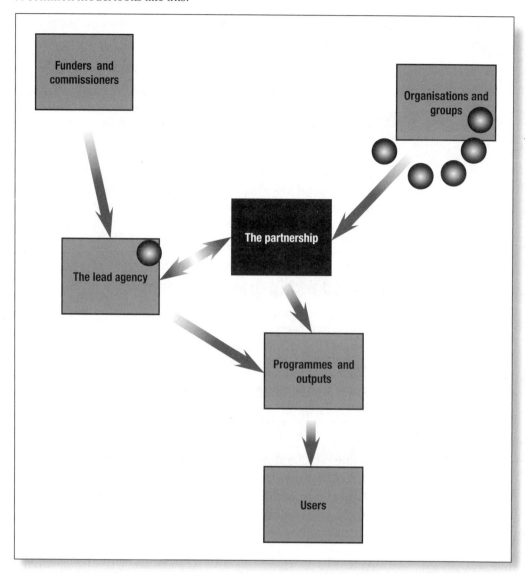

The funders or commissioners sponsor and fund the work. Often, funders are attracted to the idea of partnership working, as it shows that organisations are capable of working together, and the process might increase the output: two plus two might equal five.

The various organisations, agencies and groups have chosen to be involved in the partnership. They have agreed to attend partnership meetings and be part of it. Once the partnership begins to operate, they may be asked to deliver or manage some element or project of the partnership's work.

The partnership itself can exist in varying forms: it could be a separate legal body or an unincorporated body, not constituted as a separate identity. Some partnerships are (or intend to be) a properly constituted legal body with their own governance arrangements, public identity and brand and organisational structure. Others are much more informal alliances between independent organisations.

Sometimes, one of the organisations that makes up the partnership acts as the lead or managing body. The lead body agrees to house the partnership: it can operate under the lead body's legal structure rather than having to create its own. The lead body might agree to act as the organiser or secretariat for the partnership. It might employ the partnership's staff and manage its finances and resources; also it might coordinate and manage the various services and programmes that the partnership goes on to deliver.

The partnership might deliver projects directly into its own name, coordinated by the lead body, or it might commission some of the partner agencies to deliver projects on its behalf.

Various issues need to be carefully managed in this model. What is the role of the lead body? It is important that the role and powers of the lead body are clarified and recorded. Its role should be to support and organise the partnership, rather than to run and direct it. It should serve, rather than control, the partnership. The lead body needs to be paid for its time and resources spent on supporting the partnership. Levels of management fees for the lead body need to be agreed in advance.

What holds the partnership together? All of the partners need to know in what they are becoming involved. What is the shared vision? What is the common set of ethos or values that hold the partnership together? Is the partnership intended to be a temporary or long-term venture? The partnership needs to have a stronger base to it than simply being a mechanism to draw down money.

What happens if something goes wrong? If one partner fails to deliver or performs badly, how would the partnership deal with this? With whom does ultimate responsibility lie? What risks are shared among partnership members?

To get a partnership working, the following points have proven to be helpful.

1 Work on a shared vision

Do not assume that everyone has the same view of the intended project outcomes or end results. Time spent establishing a clear view of what the partnership is coming together to achieve will help improve communication and build on a shared identity.

2 Identify what all partners can bring to it

A good way of making the partnership work is to identify what each partner brings to it. Some partners might bring resources and expertise; others bring things which might be less tangible but are equally, if not more, important. For example, on the partnership board of a community safety project, the two representatives from the local residents' association brought an understanding of the history, make-up and culture of a local estate to the project that none of the people from professional agencies had. Their know-how and local credibility was of considerable value to the partnership.

3 Encourage joint training and sharing

Getting the people who make up the partnership to work together and develop shared experience can speed up joint working, build good communication and break down traditional barriers.

4 Allow difference

It is important to recognise that a partnership-based project is built on differences. Not everyone has to be and act the same, provided that they have signed up to the overall vision and strategy.

5 Be clear about delivery

Things do not just happen: simply because a meeting has agreed that something will happen, does not mean that it will. Systems need to be developed to ensure that responsibility for action is agreed, and that progress is monitored and chased when lacking.

6 Ensure report-backs

Make sure that people on the partnership are reporting back and involving their organisation and community. Producing simple progress notes and written project plans might encourage or remind people to report back.

7 Build in review sessions

Plan out simple review sessions. For example, one inter-agency project has six-monthly review sessions to discuss how the partnership is working, acknowledge progress and setbacks, and check that the project's processes and ways of working are supporting involvement.

8 Monitor levels of involvement

A useful exercise is to monitor occasionally the levels of involvement in the partnership. Who is participating? Who has fallen away? Does anyone have to take an unfair level of responsibility? It is also useful to identify if any key or new interests are missing from the partnership.

9 Plan for the partnership's future

As part of the review process it is worthwhile to discuss the future of the partnership. Questions might include the following.

- Should it continue in its present form?
- How might it need to change?
- Will the current membership, structure and ways of working continue to meet our needs?

Surviving partnership projects

An experienced voluntary sector worker described his experience of a working on a project established by an inter-agency partnership:

> It's very like herding cats – trying to get them all to point the same way can, at times, seem impossible. Despite what they say, they have all got a different idea of what the project is about and what it should be doing. There are lots of tensions and conflicts simmering below! Sometimes I spend more time trying to get the partnership working then I do on delivering the work.

The following six ideas can help to manage projects that come from partnerships.

Seek active agreement about the purpose

There is a danger of assuming that because individuals have attended partnership meetings, and organisations were represented, they understand and are in agreement with what the project is going to do. The process of putting together the project definition and signing it off needs to be active and deliberate. For example, one project asked each member of the partnership to go back to their organisations and discuss the intended project to ensure that they were on board and willing to support the project.

Clarify and record the structure

Partnerships need clear lines of accountability. Who will control and manage the project's resources? Will there be a lead partner, and if so, what will be the extent of their power? Who does the project leader report to between partnership meetings? Are all the examples of the kinds of issues that need to be talked through resolved and recorded?

Be sure about lines of accountability

It is useful to play 'What if . . .' games at the beginning of the partnership. Questions such as 'What would happen if we overshot the budget?', 'What if we had a major staffing problem?' and 'What if someone wanted to take us to court?' can help to test the nature of the partnership, identify risk and help people to identify individual and collective responsibility.

Carry out a mid-point review

A useful strategy is to hold a mid-point review session with all of the original partners. This meeting should revisit the original project definition, review progress and iron out any problem areas.

Keep all partners informed

There needs to be a mechanism to keep the partners informed as to what is happening in the project. People need to get the same message at the same time.

It does not have to be permanent

Often partnerships work best when there is a compelling need for individual organisations to join forces and work together. Such a need might change or vary over time, so it is worthwhile to check occasionally that the partnership is still relevant and has the support of the partners.

Managing the project

his chapter looks at the following aspects of a project:

- the start of the project
- creating teamwork
- keeping the project on track
- dealing with problems and setbacks
- reviewing the project
- moving the project on
- how to review the project's progress.

The start-up

Once the project definition, project plan and costings have been agreed, the project can start. This is the point where the assumptions and thinking behind the project are tested. Power and decisions shift from those who plan, to those who do. The project needs to change gear and begin to demonstrate that it can deliver.

The launch

Projects tend to have some sort of public launch, and this can serve some useful purposes. It can help to raise the project's profile, generate interest and bring people together to encourage them to feel part of the project. It is useful to ensure that a simple and consistent message about what the project is aiming to do goes out during the launch stage. This message can be drawn from the definition stage. It should describe, in plain language, what the project is trying to do, what it will offer and at whom it is aimed. It is also useful to use the launch to manage people's expectations and sometimes correct views of what the project can deliver.

In the launch it is important not to oversell what the project can do. For example, a manager of a housing project described how he sat through a presentation by his organisation's director of what his project was going to do:

> *It was incredible. The project was going to tackle all sorts of problems. Create real progress. Deliver amazing results. I was impressed, until I realised that it was totally over the top. I felt that we were being set up to fail!*

Creating teamwork

Few projects can be one-man or one-woman ventures. Projects need to bring in and involve other people. In the research for this book, it was interesting to find how often the managers of successful projects were facilitators or organisers of others rather than doing it themselves. As the project leader of a social policy campaign commented:

> *It was a real learning point for me when I realised that it wasn't my role to 'be the project', know everything and do everything. I see my role as getting others to be involved, create teamwork and support their contribution to the project. It might take longer and it might mean me having to give up some control, but I think that there is much more chance of the campaign being successful.*

Teams in projects can play different kinds of roles: some teams can bring in expertise or particular skills; others can give advice and support to the project manager or be involved actively in delivering the project's work.

Teams need time and support to develop. Putting a loose collection of people in a room and telling them that they are now a 'team' rather than another meeting will rarely work. Here are seven practical ways in which a project leader can encourage a group to become an effective team.

1 Clarify why they are there

Individuals need to know why they are there. What contribution are they expected to make? How much time will it take? What particular skills and expertise can they bring to the team?

2 Focus on the outcome

Members need to move beyond their individual specialism and see how it relates to the overall purpose of the project. This might involve having to push or help people to move out of their 'comfort zone': for example, getting a finance person to see, appreciate and feel part of the whole project, not only its financial aspects.

3 Project planning as a team activity

Activities such as doing a work breakdown schedule, identifying project milestones and putting a plan together can help members to understand the project and see how it all fits together.

4 Use people's skills

A useful exercise is to list the skills that are going to be needed to deliver the project, and then ask team members to identify the ones in which they feel competent. This process can help the team to recognise the skills within the team and use the resources available.

5 Agree some rules

All teams need some basic agreement as to how they are going to organise themselves. At an early team meeting it might be worth getting the team to agree some basic rules covering issues such as confidentiality, behaviour and ways of operating. Having rules that the team has developed can help to build self-discipline.

6 Get on with the work

There comes a point when a team has to stop talking about the project and get on and do it. Leaders must ensure that discussions lead to conclusions, which in turn lead to action. Work should be distributed fairly and task lists circulated quickly. A useful tactic is to ensure that every group member has a few specific things to do after each meeting.

7 Early wins

Progress creates progress. It is valuable if the team feels that it is making progress early in the life of the project. Identifying, acknowledging and celebrating a few early successes can raise morale and profile and help the team to feel that it is making a difference.

Are we focused?

In projects, people can assume that issues such as vision and values are clear to all involved. The assumption is held so strongly that no one takes responsibility for checking that there is a central unity of purpose and ethos. For example, in one relatively new agency, 13 staff, committee members and volunteers were asked to write down why they existed and what they believed was important about how the project operated. The statements were vastly different. Some thought that the aim of the project was to campaign against particular local authority policies, whereas others thought that its role was to develop long-term partnerships and close relations with the local authority.

Many of the conflicts and uncertainties that the project experienced were identified as being linked to the lack of an agreed vision for the project rather than personality clashes. The person who set up the project and chaired the committee was surprised at how little unity there was within the project. She recognised an urgent need to redefine exactly what the project was about.

Keeping the project on track

Once the project begins to roll out, it is important to ensure that it is not distorted or diverted away from its original idea.

The case of the lost vision

The coordinator of an environmental project used his skills as a systems engineer to describe how his project lost its way. In a period of 18 months, the following series of events, causes and effects happened.

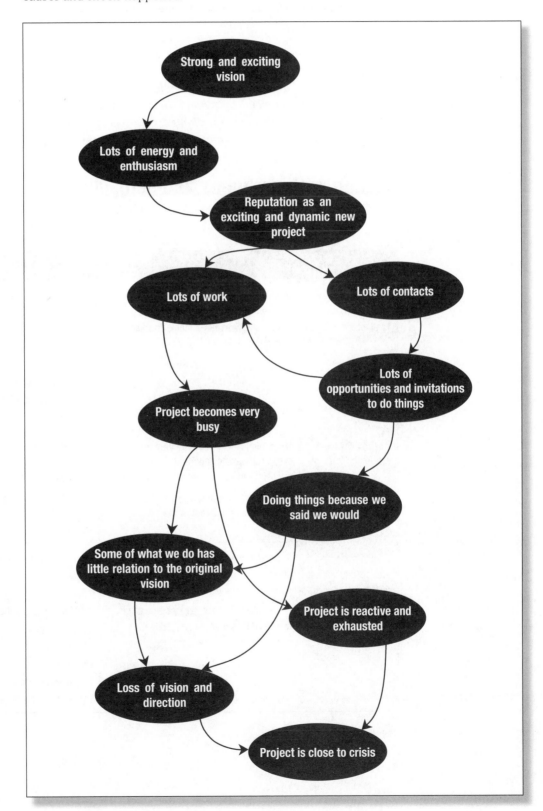

Looking back, he describes these first months:

When we launched we felt very positive. There was enormous support and goodwill for the project. Lots of people and agencies were keen to work with us. We did not see it at the time, but we became swamped by work and contacts. We took on far too much. We allowed ourselves to become involved in lots of different types of meetings and potential projects.

We were soon being driven by being busy rather than by what we wanted to do. At first it felt good to be busy. But soon we were too busy to think. We became reactive. We only did things when it was the last minute and was urgent.

We are now trying to get out of the crisis that we have created. We have to make sure that we are in the driving seat and are strategic about what work we take on. We need to develop good monitoring and evaluation systems to help us to question our work. We need to become skilled at saying 'no' and refusing to be bounced from idea to idea. Over the past six months we have been driven by urgency and activity rather than vision and direction. We must take action to restore it.

Dealing with problems and setbacks

In the life of a project, problems, setbacks and conflicts can occur. Here are some common examples and suggestions as to how they can be tackled best.

Issue	Example	Action
What we are doing is not what is wanted	Workers on a care support project soon realised that the service model they were using was not suitable in most cases.	Important to get early feedback from users. Take the initiative and use the feedback to report back to the sponsor in a positive way. Provide options and alternatives – doing nothing will probably mean that it will get worse.
Key stakeholders are losing interest	Nine months into a community arts project it was obvious that the project sponsor had moved onto other projects. Despite her early enthusiasm she displayed little interest in the project.	Ensure that there are regular project updates highlighting outcomes and success going back to the sponsor. Treat them as an investor rather than a funder – show them evidence of outcomes.
Project costs rise and/or time begins to slip	It became obvious that the project plan and budget for an education project was hopelessly wrong. It was likely that the project would miss key deadlines and go over budget.	Good monitoring systems and milestones should give an early warning. Ensure that the sponsor hears about the problem – no surprises. Take the initiative by offering a solution at the same time as explaining the problem. Focus the discussion on moving forward rather than looking for blame.

Issue	Example	Action
Mission drift	The first year of a crime reduction project was a stunning success. As a result, project workers were asked to get involved in other activities and areas which were not part of the original plan.	An agreed and recorded project definition should make clear the scope of the project. Keep returning to the definition. Avoid absorbing new work – if the requests to add things in are significant, then the project should be redefined; things should be added in only if others are taken out or extra resources are allocated.
The project has to beg and borrow resources	The finance manager of a charity which hosted a health awareness project raised concerns that the project workers were being subsidised by the charity. The workers relied upon the charity's general office staff to do their support work and regularly used the charity's resources for their project.	It is useful to agree a protocol or memorandum of understanding between the host and the project, setting out expectations and management issues. Project review meetings should review budgets to ensure that the full cost of supporting and managing a project are accurate.
The project runs out of steam	At the halfway point of a three-year rural enterprise project it was apparent that the project had hit a plateau. Fewer people were involved. The project was falling into a pattern of simply repeating what had been done before – it lacked energy.	A mid-point evaluation might provide the catalyst to review what has worked and to refocus the project. Changing the project team by bringing new people or moving people around might act as a spark.

Here are some practical ways to keep a project on track.

- **Manage communication**

  Communication does not just happen. Often there are times in a project when the project is working hard, but has little direct profile or visibility. There is a danger that people who supported it will simply forget about it.

- **Produce a regular update at each milestone**

  At each project milestone the sponsors, partners and contacts of an environmental project are emailed or given a simply produced one-page project update. The update summarises what has happened and the workplan for the next few months. The update is a useful way of reminding people of the project's work.

- **Develop the invisible project team**

  This is the network of early users, partners and supporters that the project can use as a sounding board to check out issues and overcome problems. The invisible project team can be a very effective way of keeping the project relevant and in touch with the intended users.

- **Hold regular and short project team meetings**

  Well-planned project team meetings can ensure that those working on the project are kept in touch with developments and feel that their individual efforts are part of a bigger venture. For example, a youth project held project meetings every fortnight. The meeting followed a three-part format: (1) updates and individual reports; (2) progress monitoring against the original project plan; (3) action planning of what needs to happen over the next few weeks.

- **Review the team's performance**

  An occasional review of the membership and performance of the team can help a project to move forward. Questions such as 'What works and what does not?' or 'What skills are we short of?' might lead to changes in the team membership or the way in which it works.

- **Go public on early success**

  An interesting tactic is to highlight achievements and early wins. In the first six months of an education project the project team held an event to look at what had worked and to showcase some client success stories. The project leader noted how 'people like to be associated with success, the event created a feeling that we were "on a roll". It made people want to be involved in the project.'

- **Watch out for 'mission drift'**

  It is easy for a successful project to go beyond its original definition and spread itself over too many areas. A project working with young people aged 13 to 18 was regarded as being highly effective to the extent that the statutory body that funded it asked the project to extend its scope and work with a lower age range. The project worker commented, 'With hindsight this was a mistake. We were pulled in by extra resources and were quite flattered to be asked, however, working with a younger age group required an entirely different approach that we were not really competent in. We lost our identity.'

- **Build a culture of celebration and achievement**

  Projects should encourage a working style that recognises successes and early outcomes and also acknowledges individual and team effort. Often we are so focused on what is not working that we ignore success. A working style that recognises results can help to build a strong project.

The seven stages

Project managers often refer to seven stages that projects go through. Recognise any of them?

1 Wild enthusiasm and huge expectations

  'This project will be dynamic, innovative, will solve all problems . . . '

2 Disillusionment

  'Oh, it's harder and more complex than we thought when we wrote the funding bid . . . '

3 Confusion

  'Just what exactly is it that we are supposed to be doing . . . ?'

4 Panic

  'We are half-way through and still haven't met our plans ... why does our funder keep wanting performance measures from us?'

5 Search for the guilty

  'It is all the fault of the funder/person who wrote the bid/management committee/someone else . . . .'

6 Cover up

  'If only we had another year's time/funding we would be able to show some spectacular outcomes.'

7 Promotion of those responsible

  'During my time at ... I provided strategic direction to an innovative project that produced some ... valuable learning outcomes.'

Reviewing the project

In the life of the project it is useful to schedule dates and times for regular project review sessions. These sessions can fulfil a number of purposes:

- they can iron out any issues or difficulties before they grow into major problems
- they can take stock of what elements of the project success criteria and plan have been achieved, and what needs attention

- they can fine-tune the project plan
- they are an opportunity to bring people back together and revitalise the project.

CASE STUDY

The King Street Development Project was an initiative set up to support the development of strong and sustainable community groups. The project's two staff offered a range of services, including training, advice, feasibility studies and practical help, to a range of developing and established community groups. After the project's first nine months of operating, the staff and management board completed this mid-point review.

Mid-point review – past

Looking back at the original project idea:

- do any aspects need rethinking?
- do any elements of the original idea need rethinking?
- do any original assumptions need challenging?

1 There is a strong demand for our work.
2 The original assumption was that the service must be free; some groups have the resources to pay for it or can tap into special funding.

What have we learned since the project started?

That the development process takes longer. Often it takes up to two years to get a new group up and running.

We have focused on technical and management support: finance, constitutional issues, etc. – they are important – but missed other issues such as vision and leadership.

If we were starting this project today, what would we do differently?

- Work in more depth with fewer groups.
- Explore ways in which we can get groups to learn from each other.
- Stress the importance of having a shared vision.

Mid-point review – present

What works?

- one-to-one advice work
- funding workshops
- resource centre.

What is not working well?

- day-long training courses have not recruited well.

What needs attention?

- links with other development agencies.

Mid-point review – future

Are there any aspects of the project's plan that need changing or rethinking?

Work with fewer groups for longer?

What kind of succession or exit strategy might be possible?

- operate as a social enterprise and start charging for some work
- work in neigbouring areas.

What action should come out of this review?

Eight ideas for project review meetings

1 Revisit the definition

The original project definition of success criteria and intended outcomes is a good starting point for a project review meeting. A useful approach is to have the definition document on display and ask participants to judge the performance so far against it. It is worthwhile to record any achievements and outcomes that the project has contributed to that were not in the original definition.

2 Go and see it

A housing project found it useful to hold project review meetings in the community rooms on the estate on which the project was working. Participants were encouraged to wander round the estate and see work in progress. For some of the host agency's senior managers this was an unusual experience, but it helped to give them a feel for the context in which the project was working, that no verbal or written report could do.

3 Identify early outcomes

As mentioned previously, a key question for project reviews is: 'Is it working?' Therefore, it is helpful for project workers to report on the effects of the project and the difference that it is starting to make, rather than simply giving lengthy reports of how busy they have been.

4 Ask for feedback

Any project will benefit from useful feedback. It can be positive or negative. It is important that feedback from users, partners and others is encouraged and valued at review meetings, and not met with defensiveness or hostility. Whoever leads the review meeting should avoid discussions about blame or who is at fault, and intend to try to create an atmosphere that welcomes and uses feedback.

5 Review assumptions

The staff of an access to technology project found it helpful to spend a review session going back to the assumptions about levels of demand and need which underpinned the original idea behind the project. One of the project team commented:

> *Several of the original assumptions about local people's attitude to technology and what they might want from the project were never tested or checked out. The review process gave the team a chance to go back to fundamentals and improve the project.*

6 Use milestones

Project review meetings can be linked to the milestones identified in the project plan. One agency uses completing the milestone as an opportunity to bring people together, hold a review meeting and then have a social event as way of creating teamwork and encouraging communication.

7 Allow failure

The review meeting should give a balanced view of the project's progress. The project staff should feel comfortable about reporting on setbacks, problems and things that did not work as planned.

8 Keep a record

The convenor of the review meeting should ensure that a record of the key issues and action points is made. Such notes should help to ensure that any action points are followed through, and can be very valuable as a record in the project evaluation.

CASE STUDY

The management committee of Green City Centre had been very keen to take on a three-year, two-worker project to encourage people to volunteer to take part in environmental initiatives.

Green City's director explained to the committee that although the project would be technically part of the centre, it would enjoy some independence. As director she would provide supervision and support to the project workers, and the centre would look after all of the project's payroll, accounting and administration. For this the centre would receive an annual management fee of £12,000 (14% of the project's annual budget).

For the first few months things seemed to go well. The project workers relied heavily on Green City's staff to develop contacts and identify potential volunteers and volunteering opportunities. The project enjoyed a 'honeymoon period'. The staff worked hard. The project received some very good local and regional publicity and was even featured in a government publication as an example of 'innovative good practice'. The project workers established an advisory group of local environmental activists to help shape the project's plan and provide feedback and support to the project.

Mid-way through the second year, Green City's director tabled a special item at the centre's management committee. She explained that she was becoming increasingly concerned about the relationship between the centre and the project. She identified four specific issues.

1 A style clash – Green City Centre had committed itself to bringing environmental issues into the mainstream. The director was concerned that the project workers seemed to prefer to work with a few dedicated environmental activists rather than the general public. She felt that the project could damage the strong public image that the centre had built up.

2 Potential competition for future funding – the director was concerned that the project workers and some of the advisory group were planning to make funding bids to secure future funding. Some of these bids would be to the funders to which Green City would be bidding.

3 Organisational conflicts – the centre's office manager had complained that the project workers made regular, and at times unreasonable, demands for office support. There had been instances where the project workers had ignored the centre's administrative procedures, and when challenged, they claimed that the procedures did not apply to them. The office manager claimed that the project was proving to be expensive to administer, as resources often leaked from the centre to the project.

4 A management clash – the project advisory group had started to behave more like a management committee. At its last meeting it had agreed that one of the project workers could attend a conference, despite the fact that there was no money in the budget for such an event. In addition, it had asked for a report on the project's budget and queried whether the management payment to the centre represented 'good value'.

The management committee decided to ask two of its members to work with the director to resolve these issues. Over the next three months the group did four things that resolved the situation and reduced conflict.

1 The group drafted a policy statement setting out the relationship between the centre and the project – this clarified the role of the advisory group by setting its role as an advisory one on future development of the work, but not to manage or direct the project's resources. It was agreed that the advisory group should be treated as a standing subcommittee of the centre's management committee.

2 The group convened a planning session with the project staff, some of the advisory group and some of the centre's staff to look at areas of cooperation and how the project's work fitted into the centre's overall mission and strategy.

3 The group arranged for the office manager to carry out a monitoring exercise, in order to establish the actual cost of housing the project. This simple exercise measured the centre's input into the project and the use by the project of the centre's resources.

4 The group spent some time looking at a few options for the project. They identified three possible options:

- the project could work to become an independent body – it would have its own staff and funding and would leave the centre
- the project would remain part of the centre, but have an independent identity and profile
- the centre would seek funds to carry on the work of the project at a reduced level once its current funding had ceased – the project's work would become a mainstream part of the centre.

The group suggested that all of the options needed to be tested and evaluated with a view to a clear decision being made at least a year before the project's current funding ended, so that alternative funding bids could be made.

Moving the project on

The project's journey from being a new entity to its mainstream phase needs consideration. Projects are launched with tremendous enthusiasm and confidence, and there is a lot of energy and willingness to experiment. However, at some stage it needs to move on. It needs to establish a pattern of work that is sustainable and realistic.

CASE STUDY

A health project experienced considerable growing pains in moving from being a new project to being a mainstream one. Its first two years had been full of innovation and experimentation. It developed a series of health programmes which were very popular and broke new ground. Considerable staff time went into programme development and design.

Towards the end of the second year, negotiations began with local health and social care authorities for two to three-year service contracts. The purchasing authorities were very keen on the project, but 'needed to see numbers'. They wanted to have significantly more programmes with a minimum of 10 participants. In the first two years, it was rare for the project to have run the same programme twice. It constantly redesigned, evaluated and developed its product. It took a considerable effort of will to move from developing the prototype to moving into service production. As one of the project workers stated:

> We wanted to keep improving the prototype, but really that was unrealistic. We had to find a way of delivering the programme that was cost-effective and efficient. We had to move the project on. We did not want to move away from our research and design activities. We were inclined to be perfectionists, but the reality was that we had to find a way of making the programme viable and to show that it could be delivered.

In moving the project on, the following issues need to be planned for and managed.

The project needs to consolidate

After its start-up phase a project needs to change pace. It needs to develop effective ways of organising its work and maintaining relationships, both internally and externally. Project staff should spend some time developing processes and systems that enable and support the project's work. Teams and effective committees need training and support to help them to work well. External partners, backers and contacts need to be worked with to sustain and develop their goodwill towards the project. Often, people resist consolidation: doing new things, making new plans and developing new relations seem much more exciting.

Watch out for complacency

It is very easy to become complacent once a project has started working. It is tempting to fall into routines, stop thinking and start driving on 'automatic pilot'. The project does things because 'we have always done it that way'. Regular evaluation sessions, contact with outside agencies, a commitment to learning, the involvement of new people and a constant curiosity can overcome complacency.

Prevent the project from being bounced into other things

New opportunities can emerge or circumstances change, and these opportunities and changes have to be balanced against the project's agreed strategy and plan.

Managing changes to the plan is difficult

A refusal to think about change by sticking rigidly to the original idea is likely to be perilous, whereas continually adjusting and altering the project throughout this phase could mean that it will lose its cohesion, identity, original vision and values. If changes are to be made, this should be in an explicit way by rewriting the original project strategy and success criteria, rather than incorporating them by absorption.

Think carefully about further growth

If a project is developing well it is tempting to think about expansion beyond its original base. Projects may choose to expand in size, geography or scope. Growth can be very exciting. However, when badly planned it can cause problems: it can lead to uneven development, put strain on the organisation, pull resources out of existing activities and reduce the sharpness of the project's original focus. Growth needs to be thought through. What is the project's optimum size (that is, when it is able to do what it wants to do most effectively)? Can the lessons and circumstances of one successful project be replicated in others?

Should the project aim to become permanent?

Fixed-term projects view becoming a permanent organisation as something to aspire to, and in many ways this is understandable. However, some projects are successful precisely because they are not permanent: they are focused and build up energy because their time is limited. Such success factors can be difficult to transfer into a permanent organisation. Sometimes, it is more effective to spend time early in the project's life developing strategies that will enable the project's work to be carried on or taken up by others on a longer-term basis, rather than the project spending its effort chasing long-term funding.

Think about the project's life-cycle

Projects seem to have a certain ecology: they can develop and grow fast, they reach a peak and then plateau. Unless something changes (or the project closes) the project can drift into decline, either quickly or slowly. The original energy and direction that set it up can drift away easily. Regular reviews, creative thinking and good strategic management can help to monitor where you are on the project's life-cycle. They help to plan for and think about what comes next.

CASE STUDY

Anyone who knew Pengor Arts Centre would agree that Martin had been central to setting it up. It was his idea. He had built support for it, found the building and navigated the project through a complicated obstacle course of planning applications and funding bids. He had chaired the committee from the start, but had taken on a whole host of other roles, from spokesman to caretaker. In the three months between the centre opening and the new director starting, he had also acted as unpaid director. Quite often it had looked as if the centre would not get off the ground. It was, everyone agreed, a tribute to Martin's vision and energy over three years that it had succeeded in starting up.

Sam, the new director, found the centre in good shape. She was new to the area, so Martin made a real effort to help her to settle in. They worked well together. He had plenty of ideas and contacts. She had lots of the managerial and financial skills needed to get the centre into shape, and decided to spend the first few months getting the centre organised. Several things, such as proper budget systems and basic health and safety issues, had been neglected in the rush to get it going.

In retrospect, the tensions between Sam and Martin became obvious at the second management board meeting. She presented two papers: the first set out a new budget. She asserted that the current budget had unrealistic income predictions, savings would have to be made and some projects might have to be delayed. The second paper called for a reduced programme of events: there was a danger, she argued, of doing too many things badly. It was better to do a few things effectively in the first year and then build up. Martin hurried the discussion through, and although the papers were agreed, he showed no enthusiasm for them. In the pub afterwards, he joked about how the bureaucrats had taken over.

Three months later, the treasurer of the committee met Sam at a Christmas party. At that stage, Sam had spent seven months in the job, and related that the 'honeymoon period was well and truly over'. When pressed, she explained that Martin carried on regardless. She reckoned that every week he had at least three ideas about what the centre could do. He regularly made commitments on the centre's behalf without telling her. He ignored the perilous financial situation by arguing that money always turned up for good ideas. Sam respected Martin a great deal – she just felt stifled by him. The treasurer talked to Martin about the situation. He admitted to feeling frustrated. He genuinely supported and understood what Sam was doing, but it simply was not fun anymore. Setting the project up and getting it going had been exciting, but running it was not.

Over the holiday, Martin thought about his position. In January he shocked everyone by resigning from the committee. He could not see any way that he could scale down his involvement. He did not want to be involved on the fringes of the centre, and had realised that it was time for him to move on. It was with a genuine feeling of regret that the committee accepted Martin's decision. Sam did feel a sense of loss, but felt that she could now do the things that she was paid for without being blocked.

Six months later, Martin is very busy launching a youth project. He is full of energy and enthusiasm for it – but this time he plans to start it, hand it over and then move on.

This example raises several issues about the role of the founder in a project.

- Is there a point in the project's development when the founder or original visionary needs to allow others to take over? Can they be so central to everything that they block others' development and growth?
- Are some people better at setting projects up and being innovative rather than managing projects?
- What type of structures and processes are needed in a project to review the kind of management needed at a given time? How can relationship breakdown between people be prevented? How can the different contributions from people in the project be reviewed?

How to review the project's progress
The project dashboard

A simple way of monitoring and recording a project's progress is the idea of a project dashboard. 'Dashboard' in this sense figuratively uses the idea of the panel facing the driver of a vehicle which contains the instruments and dials that they use to make decisions and adapt. In a similar way, a project dashboard should contain all the key measures for recording that the project is on track and under review.

For example, a three-year project aiming to recruit, encourage and support volunteer mentors to work with vulnerable young people developed a simple dashboard which it updated on a monthly basis. Here is the dashboard for July, halfway through the project's life-cycle.

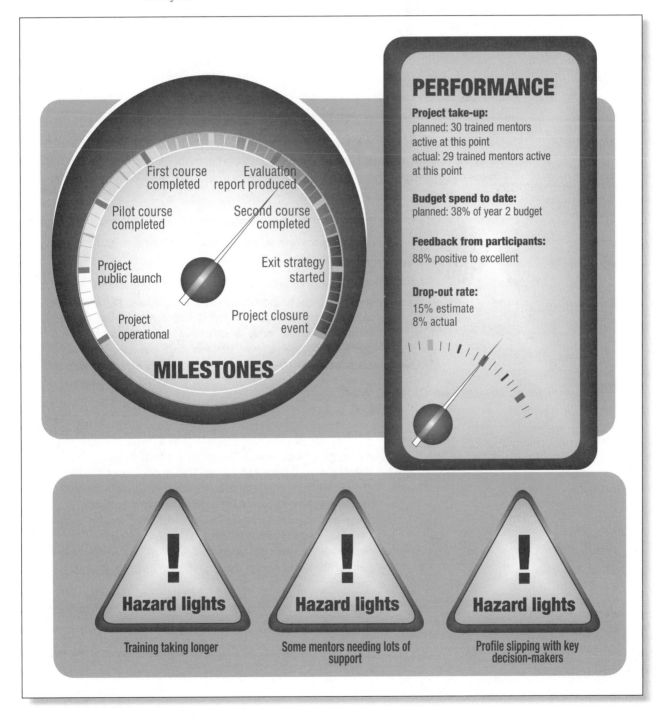

Okay ... so who does it?

Once the project is planned, the next stage is to ensure that all tasks and responsibility for them are assigned clearly to individuals. A useful tool for this is a simple matrix.

Task	Person	Sue	Bob	Terry
Organise project office			R	
Set up IT systems		R	S	
Get printer's estimates		A		R
Organise launch event		R	S	S

R = responsible for; S = support role; A = approves or signs off

One organisation found it useful to display the matrix in chart form in the organisation's office and online. The project manager commented:

Having it on show is an obvious reminder as to what should be happening and who is involved in each element of the project. It needs to be updated regularly. I have found through experience that things don't happen unless they are clearly assigned to individuals.

CASE STUDY

A manager of a regeneration agency describes how her organisation changed how it managed project review meetings:

About three years ago we instituted a policy of regular monthly project review meetings. At first they worked, but after a while they became at best a chore and at worst an ordeal! Project leaders would produce loads of information, mainly reporting on what they were doing rather than what had been achieved. Managers would then spend time asking questions. Often it was only negative issues or problems that got focused on – no wonder staff would do anything to avoid these monthly sessions. The sessions were often called the 'Star Chamber' or 'show trial'.

We have radically changed the format. We have tried to make the review process more positive. The project's success criteria and original plan are displayed on the wall. Written reports are kept to an absolute minimum. Project leaders are encouraged to give a balanced report, highlighting successes and setbacks. Managers can offer advice and support to the project leader without taking over the issue. The review meetings have helped to create a more open culture – problems and mistakes are allowed, but should not be a shock or surprise. The review process should give us early warning of project problems.

Closure and beyond

The end phase of a project can be a difficult one. The staff on the project team are concerned about their job prospects. Service users may have begun to rely on the project and are anxious about being let down. The host organisation is concerned about who will carry on the work that the project has generated.

There is a tendency to see project closure as the worst scenario or even failure. In the past, a 'good' project might be able to persuade a funder to extend its funding for another year, or even secure support to make the project mainstream as a permanent activity. Nowadays, it seems much harder to extend or make a project permanent so managers are having to deal increasingly with project closure.

Few projects can be closed neatly on a designated date: usually a level of expectation, demand or reputation has been built up which cannot be simply switched off. Most projects create some kind of ongoing demand – here are some examples.

Project work	Ongoing work
A project to design and set up a community website	Maintaining and updating the website
A campaign to recruit new members and supporters	Supporting, servicing and retaining new members and supporters
An outreach project to make contact with isolated and hard-to-reach potential service users	Meeting users' expectations

Careful and rational thought needs to be given as to what might happen at the end of a project. There are three aspects to this.

1 How will users' needs and expectations be met?

2 How can it be ensured that the expertise and knowledge which has been developed through the project is not lost?

3 How can the organisation manage closure in a way that best supports project users and project staff?

Organisations hosting projects need to develop an exit strategy or strategies setting out how the project's closure will be managed, and what will happen after the project. Other terms for 'exit strategy' include 'succession plan', 'legacy strategy' and even 'future-proofing projects'.

CASE STUDY

A bad ending

Morton Leisure Development Project was a well-planned and designed initiative. Its programme of health education and sports participation was well received, innovative and filled a much-needed gap. It had secure funds for three years, but discussions of what would happen after that time had been avoided tactfully.

Towards the end of the second year the project staff started to express concern about the long-term future. A fundraising consultant was engaged to look at how the project could be funded in the long term. Approaches to possible funders were disappointing. They all recognised the useful and creative work of the project, and the funders would like to have found a way to help, but there was little, if any, possibility of long-term or core funding. The best on offer would be occasional bits of project funding.

In the third year the tone and style of the project changed. The project leader spent most of her time looking for alternative income to continue the project. The staff felt demoralised and worried about their prospects. The level of work remained roughly the same, but the project lacked the spark that it once had. All the energy and attention went into chasing after funding rather than developing the work.

Four months before the end of the project, the staff and steering group realised that there was minimal chance of the project continuing after the three years. The best option would be to use some local authority underspend to delay the closure for a few months.

In the project's final six months, it faded away. Some staff left early. There was little enthusiasm and excitement about any of its events or activities, and the impending closure loomed large. Eighteen months on, the project has been forgotten. People have a vague memory that something about health and sport was once run. Indeed, there is now talk of creating a small project to do similar things, but called something different.

The former project leader makes the following observations on her experience:

> We denied reality. From the outset, no promise or indication was made that there would – or could – be any long-term funding. We ignored that and got carried away by our own enthusiasm. We organised our activities as if they would go on forever. It would have been better if at the start we had said what lasting difference five people with three years' funding could make. We should have seen ourselves as pilots and developers, rather than mainstream providers. We made the mistake of thinking like an organisation and not like a project. We wanted to be a permanent entity, rather than focusing on creating change.

> We should have worked towards the end. The hardest kind of fundraising is to go to someone and say: 'Our initial funding is about to run out. We will soon be out of work. We would like you to pick up the tab.' It is hardly a positive or enticing pitch. We should have put together a programme of spin-off projects, new activities and other initiatives that could have grown out of the main project.

> We should have ended on a high. It is hard to remember it now, but for the first two years the project was a huge success. It was dynamic and made a real impact locally. We lost it. We turned inwards and became focused on securing the non-existent 'holy grail' of permanent funding. Once we took our eye off the ball, we lost it.

An exit strategy should set out what will happen after the project and how during the life of the project work can be carried out to implement and secure the desired exit.

It might be appropriate for a project to have several possible exit strategies. For example, a three-year project might feel that the most desired exit would be to transform itself into a community business, in the hope of generating enough income to support its work. In addition, it might decide that if it has not developed and tested a robust business model by the end of the first quarter of the third year, it will adopt another exit strategy and an orderly closure.

Developing an exit strategy

Exit strategies are not easy. At times it is tempting to suggest that an exit strategy is a new concept used to make short-term funding sound more manageable and effective than it actually is. It implies that everything can be planned and managed to order. All the project has to do is set itself up, deliver and then move into its prepared exit strategy. However, if projects are to be short term, serious thought needs to be given to what happens when the project, or its own sources of funding, cease.

Increasingly, funders request to see exit strategies at the time when funding or project bids are being considered. At this stage it is difficult to prove that the exit strategy will work. All it is possible to show is that the project has thought about it intelligently and developed some plans. How the project closes down and what happens to its work is a question that needs to be reviewed at key milestones throughout its life.

There is a growing interest in the idea that moving into social enterprise and trading is a viable exit strategy for a project. The idea is that the project's future lies in being able to trade and sell something that will create a lasting income stream. This kind of exit strategy requires careful business analysis, including asking the following key questions.

- Does the project have a service or product which has, or could have, market value and which people would want to buy?
- Are the costs of the service fully identified? Often projects receive hidden subsidies such as cheap accommodation.
- Do we understand how the market operates? Is there a gap?
- Do we have sufficient skill to run a (social) business?
- Will we be able to manage the cultural transition from being a funded project to one that earns its income?

Whatever exit strategy is chosen, it is important that work on it begins early. Leaving it to a few months before the end will damage the project and the organisation's credibility.

It is useful to try to involve the project sponsor in the exit strategy. At one level the sponsor has a responsibility to ensure that its investment is carried on – it might have contacts and access to resources to help the project.

Managing closure

Bringing a project to a close requires organised and deliberate management action. Various factors may need to be organised, including:

- the settlement and closure of project accounts
- ensuring that staff matters are handled in line with legal and contractual obligations
- completing end-of-project reports for funders
- putting together records of the project to aid evaluation and future projects
- closing the project's offices.

In terms of bringing a project to a smooth and ordered closure, the following strategies can help.

Keep the end date firmly in mind

Plan the project's critical path so that the end date is a central focus. Be careful that the project does not simply fade away.

Use and develop the project's network

Build an invisible project team which can help to carry the work on after the project has ceased. Keep them informed and involved in the project. Towards the end they may take on greater significance.

Be willing to hand things over

Organise a gradual programme of advance briefings, consultations and training to enable other people to take on the project's work. Pilot exercises, resource materials, handbooks, contact points, follow-up meetings, on-site consultancy and user networks can help to build the confidence and skills of those who might carry on the project's work.

Look after the project team

Acknowledge possible feelings of loss: a key issue is in helping people to move on to roles and projects. One useful approach is to identify and record individual and group successes.

Record the learning

A useful exercise is to pull together all the key lessons that people working on the project have learned. As well as contributing to the project evaluation, this can help people in follow-on activities and other projects.

Celebrate: end on a high

Aim to end the project on some kind of high. A conference to share the work of the project, the production of a publication or even just a good party can help the people who have played a role in the project to feel that their contribution has been worthwhile and recognised. Ending on a positive note can create goodwill towards follow-on projects and activities.

Ten reasons to close a project down

1 It has achieved its purpose or mission.

2 Other people do the same thing consistently better.

3 The project's output is not worth the input.

4 The original assumptions, needs and driving forces behind the project have changed significantly.

5 The only purpose served by continuing would be to continue to exist as an organisation.

6 The work of the project is dogged persistently by internal conflicts and disputes that prevent work from being done.

7 It has fundamentally lost the confidence of its users and backers.

8 It is no longer financially viable and insolvent.

9 The project's resources could be used to much greater effect elsewhere.

10 Any of the above plus the lack of a critical mass of people inside and outside the project committed to turning it round.

Choosing your exit

Possible strategy	Example	Issues	Potential problems	Action needed
The project becomes permanent and self-supporting	An agency secured funding for a community café, with the plan that after two years' funding it would be able to generate enough income to be a viable community business.	Need to develop a business plan projecting the full costs involved in being self-supporting and the actions and support needed to become viable.	The true costs involved in being self-supporting are not fully recognised or known.	Need to monitor costs continually and revise projections and assumptions about what is needed to be independent.
The project is a one-off	A charity ran an anti-bullying project with three schools – it made it clear that the project would operate for two years.	Important to be clear from the outset that the project is only temporary, to avoid people becoming dependent on it.	Cynicism from some people: 'What is the point of another short-term project that will vanish into thin air?'	The project must make it clear to all users, partners and others that it is not a permanent feature – only take on what can be delivered fully.
The project is a demonstration project	A homeless agency ran an innovative project tackling youth homelessness – it built in research and evaluation time to demonstrate learning from the project in the hope that others would take it up.	Costs of research, evaluation and dissemination must be built into the project. Demonstration projects need time to show that they have been effective.	Good research and evaluation takes time, can be costly and requires independence. Danger of just producing another glossy report to sit on the shelf.	Need to plan the research and dissemination project from the outset.
The project creates partners	A health promotion project built up a network of nurses and others who could continue the work after the project's end.	The project needs to ensure that the partners have the skills, support and organisation to carry on the work.	The partners might feel that they are being pushed into taking the project on – do they have the time and capacity?	The project must put time into building up a network of partners.
The project scales down its activities towards the end	A specialist advice agency implemented a closedown plan – it stopped taking on new cases six months before the project's end date.	Needs the discipline to say 'no'. The project may need to plan what happens to staff and other resources during the closedown.	The closedown needs careful management – it can be a depressing affair.	Need to have very clear dates agreed in advance at which to implement the closedown plan.
Follow-up projects and activities are created	A neighbourhood community project created volunteer-based community groups to carry on the work and obtained resources to support the follow-on.	The project should see its key role as building the capacity for all of the follow-up activities.	Will the spin-off projects be able to operate without the input and support of the project?	The project must give a lead to help the follow-on activities to develop.
Aim for another funder to take over funding	When its three-year lottery-funded project ends, a carers' support project hopes that the local authority will take over funding.	The project must understand the lead times to which other funders work.	Funders can be reluctant to take over another funder's project. Funders prefer 'new' projects.	The project must get early support from potential funders – does the project need to be reinvented in order to attract new support?

Project papers

Sample project closure/exit plan

Use this document to set out how the project will end. It should be completed at least four months before the end of the project. It focuses on:

- managing the end of the project
- what will happen after the project – the exit plan.

Project closure

What sort of exit plan is planned for this project?
It is envisaged that organisations that use volunteers will be able to recruit, support and retain young volunteers better
The final nine months of the project will centre on developing the capacity of organisations and preparing resources that they can use after the project
Possibility of a small-scale project with the college to explore how volunteering can be developed as an access route back into education and training

What are the key steps needed to implement this plan?	What are the next steps in implementing this plan?
Support work with local agencies	Training course planned
Training and development	Resource pack in production
Resources developed	Project plan being developed with the college
Continue discussions with the college	

What will happen after the project?
Support for young volunteering will be a mainstream issue within our organisation
We will promote the resource pack and organise network meetings

What organisational tasks need attention in order to close the project?	Any outstanding contractual or legal issues involved in closing the project?
Draw up final report	Need project sponsor to sign off final report
Close budget	
Exit interviews for staff	
Create a folder of project resources	
Circulate evaluation report	
Organise end of project event	

How will the project evaluation be organised?
An end-of-scheme evaluation is being undertaken by the University of East Side
Draft report due in four weeks

Project evaluation

Evaluation can be seen as a remote and uninspiring activity. However, it should be a positive and creative exercise. Good project evaluation is:

- **more than a report**
  The evaluation process should be one that helps people and organisations to learn and develop.

- **more than data**
  Counting and monitoring a project's performance is only part of evaluation. Evaluation needs to capture people's opinions, feelings and views. Data and statistics only give part of the picture.

- **not just for the end of the project**
  Evaluation should run through the whole of the project. It should help to inform and focus the project's plan.

- **not an expert-led process**
  Good evaluation should include everyone who has been involved in the project.

A useful way of describing the evaluation process is adapted from David Kolb's (1984) learning cycle:

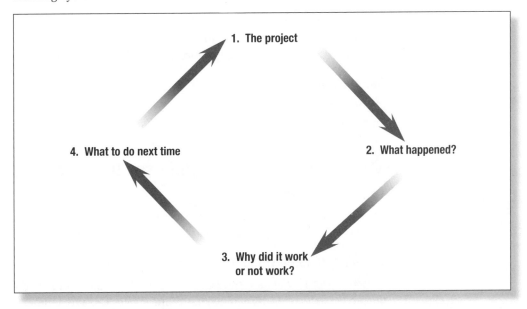

First, the project develops its plan and delivers its outputs. The second stage, 'what happened?', is about capturing evidence of what the project did, what people thought of it and what difference it made. The third stage is about analysing why things did (or did not) work, drawing conclusions and the lessons learned. The final stage is about identifying how to use and apply the experience of the project in future activities and new projects.

Some organisations spend time collecting data but rarely move on to analysing it or seeing how the lessons learned can be applied. Over the past 10 years there has been considerable interest in how organisations measure, monitor and evaluate their work. In the public sector a whole range of performance measures and indicators, reviews and studies have been developed. The director of one agency described measurement overload:

I sometimes feel that we are sinking under the weight of all these systems. I think that we will soon reach the stage where for each person working we will need to have another person monitoring and reporting on their work!

Two factors can drive the reasons why projects need to spend time on evaluation:

1   meeting the need to be accountable and report on performance
2   monitoring and evaluation for learning and development.

Meeting the need to be accountable and report on performance

These days in the public sector, politicians and managers expect regular information about the performance of projects that they have commissioned or funded. It is not enough to be doing good work – it needs to be proved.

The need to show and test value for money

Government has a strong interest in value for money and best value to show that public spending is used wisely and properly.

Measurement as a key part of the contracting process

Funding systems are moving from a grant-aid process to using contracts and service agreements that set out clear expectations of what the project will do. In most agreements the process for monitoring and evaluation is set out, and performance measures are used to judge performance and delivery.

Sponsors need to show results

Sponsors and funders need to show that they are making an impact and achieving objectives – simply showing how much money they have spent is no longer good enough.

Greater public scrutiny

Projects need to be able to produce evidence of their effectiveness to withstand an ever-increasing range of value-for-money studies, spending reviews and policy reviews.

Monitoring and evaluation for learning and development
To find out what works

Good evaluation can help a project to learn by identifying what works. It can identify the impact of a project's work, analysing which aspects are effective and which need attention.

To measure achievement

Monitoring and evaluation should show the progress that a project is making. This can help the project to focus on its achievements and successes, and demonstrate to funders, sponsors and others that the project is a success.

To develop understanding

All too often, project staff are so heavily involved in working on the project that they lack time to stand back and take a broader view. Good systems encourage people involved in the project to look at trends, identify patterns and improve their practice.

To get feedback from users

Monitoring and evaluation can be an opportunity to open up communication with a project's users. Early feedback from users can be valuable in developing future plans and identifying any problems.

To link into planning

There should be a strong link between project monitoring and evaluation and project planning. The results of evaluation should inform future plans and shape strategies.

Achieving a balance between accountability and learning can be difficult. Some funding bodies appear to be interested only in data and number-crunching rather than in the broader patterns and longer-term impact.

CASE STUDY

The coordinator of an employment project described how she tackled the project funder's narrowness:

Our main funder seems to love number-crunching. They are forever asking for statistics so that they can produce charts and graphs that are really quite meaningless: all they really showed is how busy we were.

We took a decision to continue to give the funder whatever data they asked for, but we have also had a campaign of trying to show them the effectiveness of our work in ways that cannot be represented on a spreadsheet. We have put on presentations to their board to report on key developments. We have also provided case studies showing the longer-term outcome of our work. The process of educating our funder has been a long one, but it is starting to pay off.

Defining the terms

There is a whole language around monitoring and evaluation: terms may not be defined or explained clearly by those that promote, require or use them. Here are some of the main concepts and techniques.

Performance

Performance is what gets done and what happens in a specific time. Performance measures usually focus on the project's 'deliverables' – examples might include the number of users that receive a service, or the number or volume of services delivered.

Performance measures and performance indicators

Increasingly, the terms 'measures' and 'indicators' are being used to mean the same thing, and there is no clear distinction between the two. Indicators and measures record specific elements of a project's performance. For example, a community arts project might have one measure to record the number of groups that it works with, and another measure to record the number of people participating in the project.

Quality assurance and quality standards

Standards are agreed statements of the minimum level of service that people should be able to expect from an organisation. For example, an advice project might have minimum standards for confidentiality, record-keeping, casework and internal management processes. Good quality standards should ensure that an organisation works in a consistent way. Quality assurance is the process of developing, managing and monitoring the application of standards. There are various externally awarded systems to validate an organisation's management of standards, including IS9001 and the Practical Quality Assurance System for Smaller Organisations (PQASSO).

Value for money

In the public sector, a value-for-money review should examine a project to ensure that it provides a good return for the money invested in it. A value-for-money approach is constructed around the following approaches.

- **Is it economic?**
  Does the amount of resource allocated make good economic sense? How does the cost of the activity compare with other projects or alternatives?
- **Is it efficient?**
  Is the output sufficient? If the activity was better organised, could more outputs be delivered for the same (or less) input?
- **Is it effective?**
  Does it work? Did it meet the original objectives? Are the outcomes worth the input?

Best Value

'Best Value' is a public sector review process whereby a pubic authority looks at how it organises a service or function to ensure that it provides best value. A Best Value review should compare the costs involved in a particular service with alternatives, challenge the basis on which it is currently provided, and consult with users and the community on their view of the service.

Measuring up

A project needs to develop its own performance measures and encourage project funders and sponsors to use them rather than have inappropriate or irrelevant measures imposed. A simple guide for developing performance measures is based around five stages.

1 What is the project's overall aim?

The work carried out in the project's definition stage should have clarified the intended outcomes and success criteria for the project. The measures used should relate to these aims. The use of good measurement systems can help to make the aims feel more achievable and tangible. If an aim cannot be measured, how will the project know that it has been achieved, or is even making any impact on it?

2 What values should influence the project?

All measures should be informed by the project's values. For example, a project might have agreed a commitment to work with the most isolated and excluded clients. Simply recording how many clients the project works with might not take into account the type of client.

3 What does the project want to measure?

The project needs to agree which key elements of its work need to be measured. It needs to develop a range of measures that are realistic, give a good view of the project's development and which report on the issues that are most important to key stakeholders. It is useful to ask people what they would find helpful to know about the project's performance.

4 What are the possible measures and indicators?

After listing what is to be measured, the next stage is to decide on the most appropriate and cost-efficient method of collecting the required information. The four-level approach (see below) is a useful tool.

5 How will the information be used and interpreted?

How will the measures be used after they have been collected and collated? Who will see them? It is worthwhile to think about how best the project can help people to understand the information properly, as raw data on its own can be misleading. The project needs to be able to present the information in a way that can explain the background, context and trends which might have affected performance.

Measuring on four levels

A practical way of deciding what measures to use is to structure the measurement process on four levels.

1 The project's activity or deliverables

Measures report on what the project has been doing; they are focused on the project's outputs and record the tangible work of the project. The measures here might include the following questions.

- Did it conform to the plan?
- How much was delivered?
- Was it what was specified?
- Was it on time and on budget?

2 Reaction and feedback

Measures at this level report on what key stakeholders think about the project's activities. The measures here might include the following questions.

- Any complaints or negative reactions?
- Any positive feedback or praise?
- How did users and other stakeholders rate the project?

3 The outcomes

Outcomes are the difference that the output has created or influenced. The measures here might include the following questions.

- What has changed as a result of the project?
- What significant difference has it made for the user?
- What else has happened?

4 The longer-term outcomes

Longer-term outcomes are about the real difference that the project has made. This could include the project's impact on key social objectives such as improving health or building a stronger economy. The measures here might include the following questions.

- What has been the longer-term impact of all outcomes?
- Has the outcome lasted?
- Has it made a real difference?

Measuring outcomes

The following list shows some possible ways of collecting outcomes.

- **Diaries and records**
  Using a range of tools to record milestones, learning and outcomes.
- **Monitoring policy or recommendations**
  Recording policy changes that your work may have contributed to or influenced.
- **Follow-up interviews**
  One-to-one interviews with users to identify outcomes.
- **Follow-up surveys**
  Postal or telephone surveys to gather information on progress towards an outcome.
- **Group discussions**
  Using a focus group approach to measure progress and identify what has changed.

- **Activity sheets**
  Keeping records of the work done to show the outputs and how they have influenced outcomes.
- **Feedback sheets**
  Asking users to complete written or visual reaction sheets to feed back on their positive and negative experience.
- **Third-party comments**
  Asking other people, for example other workers or the people who referred the user to the project, if they can identify outcomes.
- **Achieving pre-set goals**
  Agreeing and recording with the user some goals at the start, and at regular intervals, identifying either which goals have been achieved, or the progress made towards achieving them.
- **Practice changes**
  Identifying changes in other agencies, for example, service providers the project may have contributed to or influenced.
- **Observation**
  Noting changes in behaviour.
- **Monitoring changes in use and expectations**
  Identifying how the kinds of issues for which a user asks for support might change over time – the user's ability to tackle some issues with minimum help is an outcome.
- **Evidence box**
  Keeping a file of feedback, stories and cases that illustrate the kind of outcomes that the project is delivering.

Demonstrating outcomes

Collecting data to show outcomes is a complicated issue and can be fraught with difficulties. Here are some pointers to good practice.

Seek permission

Ensure that you have the user's active agreement to record information about them or to make contact with them at a later stage. Explain why you are collecting information and that you are monitoring the organisation, not testing the user.

Independence

People can be reluctant to give feedback (positive or negative) to an individual whom they might rely on for support. Some organisations have experimented with workers shadowing each other and having responsibility for collecting information.

Use a variety of tools

All tools are imperfect. Try to use a range of monitoring tools to collect information.

Make it easy to record

Build the monitoring system into existing office and case systems. Having a separate monitoring system can add to paperwork and feel like another chore. There is more chance of accurate monitoring if the monitoring system is built into the project.

Allow space for side-effects and unplanned outcomes

It is useful to keep the monitoring system open enough to allow for side-effects and unplanned outcomes.

Focus on behaviour

Recording changes in attitude is difficult to substantiate. A project might claim that it has developed a more inclusive approach to working with users – however, the real test is what lasting difference it makes to their lives.

Ensure that monitoring does not compromise the service

Make sure that monitoring is not seen as intrusive or could breach issues such as confidentiality. Agree how information will be recorded and ensure that users understand why and how information is being collected.

Managing project evaluation

Much of the literature about evaluation talks about two types: process evaluation and programme evaluation. Process evaluation is focused on how the project works and is organised: it looks at the ways that the project uses or has used its resources, and the effectiveness of the project's systems for planning, communication and managing. Process evaluation tends to be geared towards the internal structure and life of the project. Process evaluation might include the following issues.

- Could we work better?
- Did people feel involved in the project?
- How well does the project communicate?

Programme evaluation aims to measure the impact and lasting change that the project has made on the original need that led to the project, and is focused on the project's impact on the user. It should look at the project's outputs and outcomes. Programme evaluation might include the following issues.

- Is the project making a difference?
- Has it met need? Has the need changed?
- What have the outcomes been?

Designing a project evaluation

Why are we doing it?

A useful starting point is to be clear as to why the project is being evaluated. What will the evaluation be used for? Who will own it: is the evaluation being carried out for the project or host agency's own purposes, or is it required to meet a need that the project sponsor or funder may have?

What do we want to know?

Evaluation reports can cover too many issues and lack clear focus. A project evaluation can focus on:

- process or programme issues – should it be about how the project is organised, or about the impact and effectiveness of what the project has delivered?
- revisiting the original idea and assumptions – the evaluation can test the original ideas and thinking that underpinned the project's definition stage. Did the project fully understand what was needed? With the benefit of experience, what would we do differently?
- feedback – the evaluation can collect together the views and opinions of the different people who have had a stake in the project. What do they think of it? How do they compare it with other initiatives?

Who should do the evaluation?

The evaluation can be carried out by people working on the project or by external people specially commissioned to do the evaluation. There are advantages and disadvantages to both approaches. Evaluation carried out by people working on or strongly connected to the project may lack independence and objectiveness: they might be too close to the project to take an open-minded view. However, as they are the people who work on the project, there is more chance of the project acting on the issues identified in the evaluation. Alternatively, there are people who earn some or all of their living as external evaluators: they work as consultants, academics or freelance experts in a particular field. External evaluators should bring a level of independence and impartiality – they should not have a particular stake in the evaluation's outcome, and their independence might bring credibility to the evaluation. However, external evaluators are not cheap; their cost needs to be built into the project's budget; they need to understand the idea, ethos and values that hold the project together; and sometimes the use of an external evaluator might cause anxiety among project staff. Staff may feel that the evaluation is being 'done to them' rather than being a shared learning experience.

One possibility is to use a mixture of external and internal evaluation. For example, one project established an evaluation team made up of staff and committee members, and appointed an external consultant to work with the team. The team carried out surveys, ran interviews and focus groups and visited similar projects. The consultant advised on the process, developed the methodology, carried out some interviews when it was felt that people would talk more easily to an external person, and facilitated team sessions to produce the evaluation report.

How should we do it?

A simple process for project evaluation is as follows.

- **Establish the issues**
  Why are we doing it? For our learning and development, or for accountability?

- **Work out what needs to be evaluated**
  What are the key things that we want to find out?

- **Plan the evaluation**
  Who should do it – internal or external evaluators, or a mix?

- **Decide when the evaluation should be done**
  What sort of timetable do we need?

- **Organise the evaluation**
  Write a brief setting out the desired outcomes of the evaluation. Appoint and brief the evaluation team, agree who needs to be involved in the evaluation and gather the information. The evaluation team should collect relevant information using a variety of means: interviews, focus groups, analysis of information, comparisons with similar projects, surveys and questionnaires.

- **Analyse and interpret the data**
  This means collation of the data, and identification of key conclusions and learning points. An evaluation report is drafted, and reporting back takes place. There is discussion within the project and with key stakeholders on the evaluation findings, and the key issues requiring attention are identified.

- **Agree an action plan**
  At this stage, an action plan is drafted, with short, medium and longer-term action points for the project, host agency and sponsor. Negotiation of the action plan with key stakeholders takes place.

- **Share the evaluation**
  The evaluation is disseminated to interested parties through seminars, meetings and circulation of the report.

Making evaluation work

For project evaluation to be effective, the following six factors are needed.

1 Clarity of purpose and ownership

Everyone involved needs to understand why the project is being evaluated and how the evaluation will help to strengthen the project and its work.

2 A clear set of aims, values and success criteria

As outlined in Chapter 4, the project definition stage needs to have produced and recorded a set of aims, values and success criteria which can be used as a benchmark for the evaluation process. The absence of clear definition or vagueness in definition ('The project aims to do lots of good things for lots of people...') makes effective evaluation very difficult, as the evaluation has nothing against which to measure progress.

3 Openness and willingness to learn

There needs to be an atmosphere around the project in which people feel open to being challenged, are willing to consider feedback and are prepared to learn.

4 Involvement in the process

Experience suggests that if people are involved in designing the evaluation process and identifying the issues to be evaluated and are kept in touch with the process, they are more likely to feel inclined to learn and change as a result. If an element of secrecy dominates the process and a final report is dropped on people, it is possible that they will feel disconnected from the exercise and be unwilling to give it any serious attention.

5 Use a variety of techniques

No single technique works well all of the time. Surveys, interviews and focus groups can be used both well and badly; in addition, a single technique can be overused. It is better to use a range of techniques to gather information and identify the common points and messages that emerge.

6 Clarity about how it will be used

All too often the written report is seen as the main focus of the evaluation. While it is important, attention also needs to be given as to how to share the results of the evaluation through events, media coverage and circulation of the report to key parties. As noted previously, it is important that the evaluation report is clear enough for the project to draw specific strategies, plans and actions from it to take the project forward.

Ways of using project evaluation

As mentioned previously, evaluation should be more than a paper report. It should be an active process in which people share experience, learn and are able to use and apply the insights gained in future projects. Here are some ways in which organisations have used project evaluation in a positive way.

Showcase it

One organisation used its evaluation report as a basis for presentations to commissioners, other agencies and potential funders. It designed a one-hour workshop that focused on what had been learned and what had (and had not) worked. The organisation ran the workshop at staff events, board meetings and other forums: it was felt that it raised the organisation's profile and generated goodwill.

Share experience

A supported housing project contacted a range of agencies involved in doing similar projects and asked them to compare experiences. These meetings, called 'benchmarking', provide a valuable way of sharing experience and practice and building future collaborative working and partnerships.

Back to the start

After its mid-point evaluation, the project manager of a drugs project made a concerted effort to go back to the people who had been involved in the original idea for the project. They were reminded of the original idea and need and were then told what the project had been able to achieve. This process unlocked a level of support and was a useful way of bringing some people back into the project.

Learn from it

An evaluation can provide valuable learning and insight. For example, a community development agency encourages project staff to run a short in-house training event on the theme of 'What worked and what didn't' for other staff and volunteers. The agency stores all project evaluation reports in its resource room and encourages staff thinking about similar projects to refer to them.

Learning from mistakes

Ever tried. Ever failed. No matter. Try again. Fail again. Fail better.

Samuel Beckett

Some of the best learning comes from being able to look at mistakes, failures and what did not work in a constructive and positive way. Good project evaluation should create the space for reflection and analysis of what did not work. Such discussion can identify valuable lessons for future projects and activities.

CASE STUDY

The assistant director of a housing agency explained:

We make sure that project leaders are encouraged to talk about what went wrong. Often the original idea or assumptions that we had were faulty or based on untested ideas. For example, we ran a project targeted at a particular community who traditionally have not used our services. Despite very hard work, the project did not work. The numbers were disappointing. It did not really produce the outcomes we intended. However, we ran a series of evaluation meetings to analyse what happened. We revisited the original idea, got feedback from the communities and encouraged the project workers to reflect and think about their experience.

From these meetings we have learned an incredible amount. We are now developing some ideas for new projects. We have also taken the initiative, and went back to the project funder and presented to them our experience and learning. For us, the real outcome of the project has been organisational learning.

Crucially, you have to get the atmosphere right. Often when there are problems, people's first reaction is to personalise it by looking for someone to blame. This often becomes destructive. We need to be clear that things can and do go wrong – I am more worried about the people who don't make mistakes, as usually they don't do anything at all.

Ten useful questions for a project evaluation session

1 What would we do differently?

2 What was different from what we expected?

3 What was harder than we expected?

4 What was easier than we expected?

5 What else happened? What side-effects happened?

6 Who were the people whose support we needed?

7 Why did the things that worked, actually work?

8 What do policymakers and funders need to understand about this kind of work?

9 What could we have done to make the project more effective?

10 If we were doing this project again, what key lessons would we apply?

Watch out for side-effects

A project's most useful outcomes can be the things that happen alongside it. A good evaluation process should pick up side-effects.

CASE STUDY

A community drugs project spent a year working with young people on an estate. The project measured its work in terms of how many young people it worked with, the number of families supported, the number of awareness sessions delivered and so forth.

Towards the end of the project it was pointed out that the way the project was working was different from other initiatives: it had convened a partnership group to advise and support the project. The group was made up of the main local agencies — neighbourhood police officer, doctors, headteacher, youth worker and social services. Through the skilled facilitation of the project leader, the group had been a success. For the first time ever, people had worked together and shared their experience. In fact, the group had agreed to continue working together after the project had ended.

Although not deliberately set out in the project's plan, this represented a significant positive outcome for the project.

Project measures and indicators

All of these measures and indicators can be used to measure and report on different aspects of a project's performance.

Measure/indicator	Description	Examples	Comments
Unit cost	The total cost of the project divided by the number of times that it is used or by the number of users.	The total cost of a community safety project was £45,000. Over the year the project worked with 182 users, therefore the unit cost was £247.	Unit costs give a very raw figure – they only make sense if the unit does not change much and requires the same level of input and time.
Overheads and management costs	The amount spent on administration and infrastructure costs as opposed to direct delivery of services.	A project was able to show that it only spent 12% of its income on administration and management functions.	Some funders are reluctant to pay for management or admin costs. Need to show that management costs are reasonable and that the management function adds value to the project.
Take-up rate	Data on the number of times that the project is used.	A telephone helpline measured the number of callers.	Really only shows how busy the project is – need also to show quality and effectiveness.
Performance against an agreed standard	Recording compliance with pre-set standards of minimum practice.	A community care project had standards setting out minimum levels of response times for people needing its services. It monitored performance against the standards.	Often used as part of a quality assurance process to demonstrate that the project works to best practice standards.
Performance against an agreed plan	Recording completion of pre-set objectives and plans.	A community development project produced a quarterly report listing progress against the targets and objectives set in the project's workplan.	The plan needs to have some flexibility to allow for events, demands and things that cannot be predicted.
User feedback	Collation of user opinions, reactions and comments.	Recording positive and negative feedback from people who use the project, based on complaints, reaction sheets and surveys.	Often hard to get feedback from users. Who collects the information can be an important issue.
Case audits or sample checks	Checking that work has been properly carried out.	A health project monitored one in ten cases to ensure that they had been managed in line with agreed policy.	The project must have clear standards of what is the expected level of good practice.
Follow-up reviews	A measure of the longer-term impact of the project.	An employment project kept in touch with a sample of former trainees to monitor their progress.	Often used to measure outcomes as well as outputs. Can be time-consuming and needs good systems to track users once they have moved on from the project.

Measure/indicator	Description	Examples	Comments
Matching expectations with experience	A comparison of what users expected and what the project delivered.	A training project developed an evaluation programme whereby participants recorded their hopes and expectations of the programme. The statements were used at the end of the project to identify progress and achievements.	Can be useful for measuring people's progress. Need to recognise that people's needs and expectations change.
Policy measures	Recording the action taken to ensure that key policies are implemented.	A project reports on what it has done to put into practice key policies on equality and user involvement.	A useful way of ensuring that policies are not just paper commitments.
Referral indicators	A measure of the route by which users were referred to the project.	A youth project monitored which agencies were referring young people to the project.	Analysis of referrals can produce useful information on the project's marketing, external relations and the use made of it by other agencies.
No service given	A measure of the occasions that the project has not been able to provide users with a service.	A community development project keeps a log every time it has to turn down a user – either because the project is at full capacity, or because the requested service is not within the project's remit.	Often this information is never collected or collated as people are simply turned away. This measure can help a project identify unmet demands and gaps.
Lost opportunities	Recording opportunities that were missed because the project did not have the capacity to respond to them.	An opportunity cost happens when a project does not have the resources or time to respond properly to an opportunity. A housing project was unable to become involved in an estate renewal initiative because all staff time was fully committed.	A useful measure to help in future planning and ensuring that the project is able to respond to new or changing demands.

The project-based organisation

This final chapter looks at the implications of the increased use of projects by voluntary organisations. It suggests some of the larger implications of being project-based, offers some advice for funders, looks at some of the organisational issues and provides some ideas on what is needed to survive projects.

The increased use of projects is driven by several factors:

- funders and commissioners operating to tighter criteria
- the need to show that an impact is being made
- greater targeting of resources.

Working with projects requires a change in how organisations think and plan work. At times, organisations have adopted strategies to cope with the uncertainties of fixed-term projects. One manager explained her strategy and its limitations:

> *I spend a lot of my time dressing things up as projects that are really long-term services. As the project comes to an end I then put in bids for 'new, dynamic and innovative' projects that look remarkably similar to one we have already been doing. I have reached the conclusion that we can't carry on in this way.*

Projects require a shift in how we organise and plan our work. A key task is to work out what the central core activities are and the kinds of things best suited to being project-based. Organisations need to be able to think and plan beyond the limitations of a two or three-year project.

Funders and projects

The head of unit in a local authority that commissioned and funded voluntary organisations described the authority's attachment to projects:

> *Project funding works for us. It gives us the ability to direct resources where they are most needed and not just fund organisations because we have done so in the past. Increasingly, we think in terms of programmes and project delivery rather than funding organisations. Organisations need to be able to show that they can start up projects and deliver outputs and outcomes.*

Organisations that commission and fund projects need to think through the implications of being project-based. In the research for this book, four specific issues were identified.

1 Projects need a strong infrastructure

Sometimes funders give out contradictory messages. On the one hand, they expect good management and want to see that there are sound and robust procedures and systems, but on the other hand, they are reluctant to pay a reasonable or fair contribution to the costs involved in managing and supporting the project. Organisational overheads ensure that projects are able to operate effectively. They are not an extravagance.

2 Outcomes need time

In many ways the interest in outcomes is a positive one. It should focus discussion on the vision and the difference we make. However, real and lasting outcomes take time and cannot be pushed into a fixed timespan. For example, as a worker in a health project explained:

> *If we wanted to, we could rig it so that it looked as if all of our clients were achieving real outcomes within a year of coming to us. In truth, all that would happen is that the same people would reappear a few months down the line because the 'outcome' was only a temporary fix.*

3 Funders need to think about the exit strategy

As sponsors of projects, funders need to be involved in planning and managing what happens after a project. The responsibility for carrying the work forward cannot lie only with the project.

4 Not everything can be a project

Some needs and services need a longer-term investment. Dressing them up as a fixed-term project denies the reality that some needs are long term and will outlast projects.

Organisational implications

Designing and operating an organisation capable of starting and managing projects challenges many of the traditional ways in which organisations have been designed to operate. As mentioned in Chapter 7, project-based organisations need to be able to adapt quickly to change and organise resources to get the best out of a short-term initiative, whereas much of the thinking which has underpinned traditional organisational design has been about designing for long-term stability and strict demarcation of specialisms and functions. Many organisations have drifted into being a collection of projects, as the following case study demonstrates.

CASE STUDY

The chief executive of an environmental agency described her experience:

Over the years we have become increasingly project-based. We have added on various roles and functions by winning resources to run projects that extend and develop our core work. We have a range of education projects, outreach and specialist projects that have tested and challenged how we operate. Staff need to be able to move from project to project. Our organisational systems need to be able to deal with an organisation that is constantly reshaping and changing. We also need to make time to be much more strategic and able to plan projects from start to conclusion, and be able to work out what happens after the project.

Building the project-based organisation

Based on research for this book, here are four features which can help to create a project-based organisation.

1 A strong core

At the heart of the organisation there needs to be an infrastructure which can perform a number of key functions:

- a sound base for projects – providing administrative support, back-up and practical support to enable projects to be effective

- connecting projects – linking different projects
- ensuring that all of the projects relate to a shared organisational vision and core ethos
- coordinating and planning – taking an overview of each project, helping it to plan, dealing with critical issues and ensuring that its work is sustained in the longer term
- a strategic role – identifying opportunities for projects and ensuring that through good evaluation, key lessons are learned and shared.

The core of a project-based organisation is much more than an administrative overhead.

2 Financial management

Organisations which are project-based need financial systems that reflect the way in which projects are created and operate. For example, the finance manager of a development agency described his role:

Our increased reliance on projects has meant three main changes for the finance function. First, we have to have very accurate systems to work out the real full cost of the project. Adding 10% of the project cost on to cover management costs is no longer good enough. We have to be much more thorough about establishing the full costs. Secondly, I have to play a bigger role in helping to put together project bids and plans. This often requires me to be unpopular and stop the organisation [from] taking on projects that are unsustainable or will never cover their costs. It is now part of my role to challenge the assumptions behind project plans to ensure that we do not commit ourselves to things that we later regret. Thirdly, our financial management systems have to be responsive and up-to-date. The days when the budget ticked along from April to April with little change have gone. We need to be able to rework our budget as projects come and go. Managing cashflow and coping with many more income streams is increasingly important.

3 Staffing

Projects usually mean an increased use of fixed-term contracts and greater flexibility in employment. The management writer Charles Handy (1989) described how many organisations were becoming what he called a 'shamrock organisation'. He described three elements:

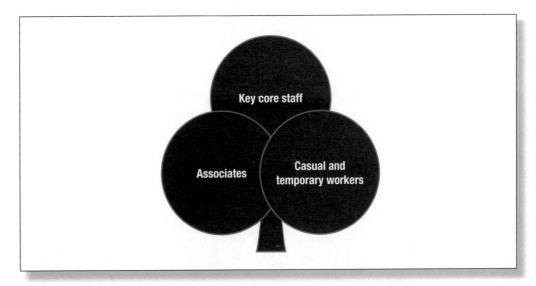

In this scenario, the key core staff are permanent: they coordinate the organisation, develop and implement its strategy and bring continuity to it. Various functions are outsourced to associates who bring specialist expertise and skills as and when needed on a contracted or retained basis. The bulk of the workforce are casual or temporary employees recruited to deliver work as and when required.

The manager of a youth agency explained how her agency had developed into a 'shamrock organisation':

> *The bulk of our face-to-face work with young people is carried out by staff working on a vast range of sessional, fixed-term and temporary contracts. Many of them have worked for us for years. Having a network of staff enables us to take on new projects quickly and be flexible in quieter times. Increasingly we rely on consultants, freelancers and specialist agencies to deliver such things as project evaluation, human resource advice, media advice and technology support. Being able to pull these things in as and when needed gives us some flexibility. At the heart of the organisation is a core team. Our role is to oversee things, coordinate and think ahead. We never design it this way. We have evolved into it.*

Managing this kind of organisation brings a whole set of challenges.

- How can consistency and a shared sense of values be maintained across an organisation which can feel quite temporary?
- How can the organisation support, train and develop workers employed on a casual basis? How can they be supported?
- Is there a danger of being too reliant on expertise that is located outside of the organisation?
- How do the core staff develop an organisation-wide identity and vision?

4 Strategy

Project-based organisations need to be adept at developing and acting in a strategic way. This is more than writing a plan: the organisation needs to be able to see beyond project timelines. It needs to be able to think in the longer term, spot gaps, needs and opportunities and work with potential sponsors. Much of this involves being able to influence sponsors and aligning an idea for a project with the sponsor's needs and funding availability.

A collection of projects

Sam's first few weeks as director of a neighbourhood development agency were spent trying to get to know the agency and its various activities. It soon became apparent that the agency had grown through taking on projects. It was obvious that Sam's predecessor had been good at grabbing funding and developing new projects.

Sam reflected on how the agency operated; it felt more like a loose collection of projects than an organisation. Sam identified four main issues.

1   Many of the staff had a stronger relationship to their project than to the agency. Several of the projects were keen to promote the identity and profile of the project rather than the agency. A recent leaflet from the childcare project made no reference to the agency.

2   Staff often failed to keep people in touch with developments and plans in their project. Communication between projects was poor: 'The left hand didn't know what the right hand was doing.' The contacts and expertise built up by one project were never passed on to other projects.

3   If a project worker was away from the agency, no one was able to cover for them. All queries about a specific project could only be answered by the project worker.

4   Several staff expressed concern about job insecurity. Most of the staff were on fixed-term contracts that would come to an end when the project ended. For many, this was demoralising and caused anxiety.

Sam realised that there was little alternative to being project-based, and set about a series of organisational reforms to improve how the organisation coordinated projects.

Four months later, progress had been made. Sam tried to get workers to see that the agency was more than just an administrative overhead for the projects. She began to ensure that all project workers had proper supervision, attended agency-wide staff meetings and developed common publicity campaigns. All of this showed in practical terms how the 'agency adds value to the projects'.

Sam also instituted a programme of staff meetings where project workers took turns to run a 'teach-in' about their project. It helped to open up communication and helped people to make connections.

The agency also set up a small staff development programme, which consisted of two elements. First, it ensured that staff learned from the project in which they were involved – this included helping them to recognise and record the skills and experience they had developed. Second, the focus was on career and job development aimed at helping to prepare staff for what would happen when their project ended – this included career advice, help with job applications and, in two cases, helping staff whose projects were coming to an end to transfer to new projects within the agency.

Sam commented:

> None of these things are that hard to think up or do, but if we had not acted, the agency would have become a very vague and loose collection of isolated projects. It's the role of the organisational core to connect all the bits together and ensure that the organisation is cohesive.

Nine practical ways to survive projects

1 Common language

The organisation needs to develop a simple and shared language and process for managing all projects. Having clear terminology about issues such as milestones, outcomes and project sponsors will help to improve communication and create better role clarity.

2 Always develop new projects

The transient nature of projects means that organisations need to be thinking about what they want to do next. Time needs to be allocated to developing new ideas for projects. As a worker in a community arts organisation said: 'You have always got to be thinking about your next project – however busy you are!'

3 Share all project plans

Project plans should be open documents. They should be updated regularly to show what progress has been made and to highlight potential problems or delays.

4 Build the core

Project-based organisations need a strong and permanent organisational centre. Core functions are more than just administration and management costs: the core should be able to link projects, provide guidance and support, and ensure that the work and lessons learned from fixed-term projects are carried through.

5 Skills and knowledge as an asset

When we prepare a balance sheet we normally think of assets as tangible things such as tables and chairs. However, often the real value in an organisation is its expertise, skills and knowledge. These assets need to be identified and managed, as they represent the actual value that an organisation adds to current and future projects.

6 Manage cashflow

Project-based organisations need to be able to cope with different income streams and projects stopping and starting. Coordinating the movement of cash becomes a demanding task, as each project is funded in different ways.

7 Connect projects up

Individual projects should not become isolated within the organisation. It is important that projects are coordinated to ensure that resources and expertise are shared, and that actions and activities are synchronised to avoid duplication or confusion.

CASE STUDY

The director of development agency described how his organisation found a way of coordinating the different projects that the agency managed:

We can regularly have between six to nine projects up and running at any one time. About a year ago I realised that it was descending into chaos. Projects were competing against each other for attention and space. Events were clashing. At one stage, three projects were all trying to get media coverage in the same week.

We have developed a system where our office manager acts as a projects coordinator. All project plans are displayed on a single Gantt chart in the general office. She negotiates with staff to ensure that projects don't all clash or all require admin support at the same time. She also liaises between projects to ensure that we coordinate activities. The role requires varying degrees of organisation, diplomacy and sometimes that ability to 'bang heads together' to ensure that the left hand knows what the right hand is doing.

8 Flexible jobs

Few organisations are in a position to be able to offer the same job for life or a safe career structure. A project-based organisation can help staff to identify the skills and knowledge that they have developed by working on a particular project, and to help them transfer that expertise to new projects as they come online.

9 Learning as a core value

Project-based organisations need to value and put resources into individual and organisational learning. Learning can open the organisation up to ideas for new projects and help people to apply their skills in a new context. As the coordinator of a children's charity described:

We are learning all the time, it is more than just going on courses. We have to find ways of identifying what we have learned from the experience of different projects and how we can take it forward. Learning keeps us sharp and receptive to change.

Ready for projects?

This exercise is designed to identify strengths and weaknesses and help organisations to develop.

Organisational feature	Description	Your assessment: 1 = serious gap 4 = meets up
1 A clear organisational vision and strategy	Strong agreement about organisational identity and purpose Agreed future direction and priorities	
2 An organised approach to project management	Common and practical systems to design, plan, manage and monitor projects	
3 Flexible structures and ways of working	Able to host new projects and provide quality organisational support to projects	
4 Robust costing and planning techniques	Accurate and sound systems to cost projects fully Practical systems to plan out a project	
5 A strong and permanent core	An organisational centre that links all the projects and ensures that all projects contribute to the bigger picture	

Further reading

Association of Chief Executives of Voluntary Organisations (ACEVO) *Funding Our Future*, ACEVO, 2001

Briner, Wendy, Geddes, Michael and Hastings, Colin, *Project Leadership*, Gower Publishing, 1996

Handy, Charles, *The Age of Unreason*, Harvard Business School Press, 1989

Jewkes, John, Sawers, David and Stillerman, Richard, *The Sources of Invention*, St Martin's Press, 1969

Kolb, David, *Experiential Learning*, Prentice-Hall, 1984

Mintzberg, Henry, 'The Rise and Fall of Strategic Planning', *Harvard Business Review* (Jan/Feb), 1994

Osborne, Stephen, *The Once and Future Pioneers*, Joseph Rowntree Foundation, 1994

Other books by Alan Lawrie

Developing Your Organisation, Directory of Social Change, 2000

The Complete Guide to Business and Strategic Planning, Directory of Social Change, 2007

Lawrie, Alan and Mellor, Jan, *The Complete Guide to Surviving Contracts*, Directory of Social Change, 2008

Index